DUEL FOR THE SKY

DUEL FOR THE SKY

FIGHTER PLANES AND FIGHTING PILOTS OF WORLD WAR II

by

Herbert Molloy Mason, Jr.

GROSSET & DUNLAP
A FILMWAYS COMPANY
Publishers • New York

For
SQUADRON LEADER JOCK HERON, RAF,
who provided the author with a
richly rewarding experience in
flight in an F–105.

Photo Credits: Peter Bowers, 1, 2, 5, 6, 8, 10, 13, 15, 18, 19, 20; David
Cooke, 21, 30, 48, 53, 60, 71, 122, 123, 132, 137, 139; Royal Air Force,
24, 25, 26, 33, 34, 36, 64, 66, 70; United States Air Force, 28, 32, 39, 46,
47, 74, 77, 78, 79, 82, 84, 87, 88, 89, 90, 92, 95, 96, 98, 100, 102, 103,
104, 105 (left), 106, 108, 115, 116, 117; Royal Canadian Air Force, 50,
56, 68, 69; Canada National Defense, 42; United States Navy, 118, 121,
125, 126, 127, 128, 130, 133, 136; Douglas Aircraft, 58; Colonel H. M.
Mason, 41, 45, 105 (right), 112, 114; Robert D. Loomis, 124, 131.

CONTENTS

The author is indebted to a number of people for help in supplying information and material that appears in this book. I am especially indebted to an old friend, Colonel William T. Coleman, Deputy Chief, Public Information Division, Office of the Secretary of the Air Force; Lieutenant Colonel Gerald M. Holland, Magazine and Book Branch, SAFOI; Captain Monte Blues, SAFOI, and Lieutenant Commander Kenneth W. Allison, Head, Magazine and Book Branch, Department of the Navy.

For help in locating official USAF combat photographs, I owe thanks to Mrs. Frances Lewis and Miss Susan Chapman, Det. 5, AAUS in Arlington, Virginia.

Illustrating these pages with rare and seldom-seen photographs would not have been possible without the unstinting labors and unselfish loan from the collections of David C. Cooke, at one end of the country, and from Peter M. Bowers, at the other.

Another kind of debt is owed to all of the fighter pilots the author has known and flown with throughout the years.

For permission to quote brief passages from published works, the author is grateful to:

Little, Brown and Company, Boston, from *My Island Home,* by James Norman Hall, © 1952 by Estate of James Norman Hall.

Random House, Inc., New York, from *The Look of Eagles,* by John T. Godfrey, © 1958 by John T. Godfrey.

MacDonald and Company, Publishers, Ltd., London, from *Fighter Over Finland,* by Eino Luukaanen, © 1963 by Eino Luukaanen.

And the author offers his appreciation to Martin Caidin, Barron Dennis, and Dan Meyer for loan of rare materials.

Herbert Molloy Mason, Jr.
San Antonio, 1970

PROLOGUE: THE HERITAGE

ON THE DAMP, cold morning of November 11, 1918, more than fifteen hundred days of attritional warfare ended in northern France. Ten million European, Asian, and North American men lay dead on the battlefields, national treasuries were in ruins, and more than one empire-dynasty was toppled forever.

How surviving warriors felt when the guns fell silent was summed up by a thirty-year-old American aviator from Colfax, Iowa, named James Norman Hall. He had seen much of the war, in the mud and in the sky. An early volunteer with Kitchener's British army in Flanders, Hall later flew as a pursuit pilot with the famed Lafayette Escadrille and then with the 94th Squadron, U.S. Air Service. After Captain Hall was shot down behind the German lines he was hospitalized and then imprisoned at Landshut. From there, he and a few companions took advantage of the chaos that erupted in Bavaria when the Armistice was signed and made their way back to France via Switzerland. Of course they zeroed in on Paris, Mecca of Allied fighting men—especially those who wore wings. Hall clearly remembered his feelings:

"Bitterness, sorrow, even mourning for the millions dead, seemed to have been put aside, for the moment at least. I doubt whether in all European history there had ever before been a time when the hearts of men were so filled with serene hope for the future; and I believe this was true not only in Paris but also throughout the entire Western world. The war that was to end war had run its appalling length. . . . And everyone—all common folk at least—believed that the opportunity could not and would not be lost; that they would see the new world beginning to emerge from the ruins of the old: one in which oncoming generations were to be freed forever from the threat, or even the thought, of war.

"That was a happy time, if ever there has been one in human history. . . ."

Hall nourished a rare desire after returning to Paris: to fly, for the last time, the entire stretch of the old Western Front. He needed, in the expression of the French, "a bath of solitude." General Mason Patrick, Chief of U.S. Air Service, granted Hall's request. From ranks of hundreds of factory-fresh Spad fighting planes—later to be burned in the "million-dollar bonfire" because they would no longer be needed—Hall chose a new 180-hp airplane and started his lonely odyssey. When he passed over the silent ruins of the village of Souain he was conscious of "a quickening of pulses, and instinctively began to look in all directions, overhead, behind, and beneath for the presence of enemies. It was all but impossible to realize that one could now fly anywhere, in perfect safety."

Hall was alone in the sky, seeing no other airplanes, hearing no other sound in "the stillness of that gray winter world." As Hall's Spad rushed over the devastated earth below, his thoughts turned to the pilots who had flown in the same sky during all the long years that lay behind. "Young men, high-spirited, loving life, of reckless courage whatever their nationality; the best of them dead: Guynemer, Richthofen, Lufbery, McCudden, Ball, Dorme, Victor Chapman, Kiffin Rockwell, James McConnell—hundreds more." Hall was thinking of men who became legends in their time.

Once Hall landed at an airdrome to replenish his fuel supply. The place, blown with snow, was abandoned except for a few elderly *poilus* huddled around a fire in front of a hangar. Seeing Hall climb out of the Spad and approach through the mist, one of the grizzled veterans remarked to his friends, "*Voila!* The last war pilot. There will never be any more of them."

And that is what they believed.

The skies of World War I bred a new kind of hero: the pursuit pilot. He was seen by the public as a goggled knight flashing through the air two and three miles above the slime of the trenches seeking mortal combat. While on leave in Paris or in London, the aviator was pictured as a dashingly uniformed, usually well-educated, generally handsome *bon vivant* with an eye for fashionable ladies and cultivated tastes in really fine wines and truly great cuisine. These men who flew the single-engined, single-seater biplanes, triplanes, and monoplanes were, above all, gentlemen. Gentlemen killers, yes, but they almost always gave the other chap a sporting chance for his life. There are many cases on record of a pilot on one side or the other breaking off combat when his adversary was seen to have run out of ammunition. It was common practice to escort a captured enemy airman to your own airdrome and there give him a proper binge before sending him off to some prison camp. One of the largest and most circumspect military funerals ever held for a dead aviator on the Western Front was given to Manfred von Richthofen by members of the Royal Flying Corps and the Australian army when he was shot down over the Somme—and von Richthofen had killed more than a hundred British airmen.

Scores, i.e., kills, of the aces on both sides were relentlessly totaled and published in daily newspapers; thus every schoolboy could follow the fortunes of the various aces. The names of the greatest pilots were truly household words, as familiar as the stars of the entertainment world and usually better known than the names of lesser world statesmen. Why? Because the First World War was an emotional experience in the deepest sense and the people at home, burdened with loss and weariness, welcomed a focus for the nameless heroism and sacrifice that war demanded. The pilots were a new breed of warrior, a relative handful when compared with the gray masses of infantry and artillery. Flying itself was still an awesome undertaking that somehow seemed to flout the gods, hinting at high adventure and a breathless sense of freedom. Every flight, every combat, was meticulously recorded in squadron logs. Correspondents sought out these pilots at the Front and while they enjoyed precious days or hours on leave. The story got told, and when reported by honest journalists was told very well.

But who could imagine reporting, "Gunner Schwartz this morning fired a 77-mm round that wiped out thirteen British staff officers in a dugout near Beaumont-Hamel. This brings Schwartz's score since 1915 to 850 killed." Or, "Sergeant Herbie Atkins, machine-gunner of the East Lancs, today raised the number of enemy dead accounted for to sixty-three when he traversed his Vickers gun across a German working party to the rear of Hill 60."

Pilots of the 1914–1918 war deserved every line published about them. The craft they flew flamed easily, there was no armor protection for the pilot, and, except for the Germans late in the war, there were no silken angels with which to float safely to earth to escape roasting or maiming. They pioneered a new form of tactical warfare, and to this day are best remembered for reviving a word not associated with combat since men wore armor. That word is "chivalry."

DUEL FOR THE SKY

Heinkel 111B–1, flown by German pilots of Condor Legion, unloads cargo of death on Spanish earth.

1 / SPANISH SKIES

IN THE SUMMER of 1936, the world spun to the edge of total war, although this was not clear to everybody at the time. A revolt exploded throughout Spain that quickly became bloody civil war. It was a revolt of the Nationalists, identified with fascism, against the Loyalists, whose followers became identified with communism.

Spain's agony was seen by Germany, Italy, and Russia as a wonderful opportunity to test their own front-line aircraft in actual combat. The Germans and the Italians not only sent their best fighters and bombers, they included pilots, navigators, and mechanics as well. These men, Hitler knew, would return to Germany with priceless combat experience which would be invaluable for the larger war that the leader of the Third Reich believed was inevitable.

The Germans and the Italians contributed more than 1,000 warplanes to the Nationalists, while the Soviet Union shipped approximately 300 aircraft to the Loyalists. The Germans fought with the highly organized Condor Legion that included, by 1938, four squadrons of the fast Messerschmitt Bf 109 monoplane fighters, two squadrons of Heinkel 51 biplane fighters, three squadrons of Heinkel 111 and Dornier 17 twin-engine reconnaissance planes, and a dozen squadrons of Heinkel 111 bombers and Junkers 52 transports. The youthful members of the Condor Legion expressed their feelings about serving Franco's cause in Spain in a marching song typical of the Nazi propaganda mill: "We shall be marching onwards, if all else crashes about us. Our foes are the Reds, the Bolshevizers of the world."

The Russians did not send organized groups of flyers to Spain, but they did train Spanish pilots inside the Soviet Union and returned them to fly for the Republicans, as the Loyalists were sometimes called. Many of these pilots flew Russian-made Polikarpov I–16 radial engined monoplane fighters,

1

Russian-built I–16 fighter was used by Loyalist pilots, including American volunteers, against Franco's superior air power.

broad, stubby airplanes that resembled Jimmy Doolittle's famous Gee-Bee Thompson Trophy racer of 1932.

The American government not only refused to take sides in the Spanish Civil War, but passed laws prohibiting shipment of any kind of help to Loyalists or Nationalists—and this law of embargo included medical supplies. But the let's-pretend attitude of the government had no effect upon thousands of Americans who felt wholly in sympathy with the Loyalists; so much so that they made their way to Spain to fight against the forces of Franco. Many of them were pilots. Among these experienced aviators was a man named Orrin D. Bell, who had flown Sopwith Camels during World War I. Bell, like the rest of the world, wondered what the new air war would be like.

At first the outnumbered Loyalist Air Force was badly disorganized, and Bell spent his first weeks in Spain doing little more than sitting around the airdrome during the day and going into the nearby town at night to dine and drink. Then Bell was ordered to the Madrid front to join a new squadron freshly equipped with the Russian I–16 fighters. Bell made his way to a hotel in Madrid where he was welcomed by several other Americans, including Tex Allison, graduate of the Naval Academy at Annapolis, and Harold "Whitey" Dahl. These veterans had as squadron mates, pilots from Switzerland, Mexico and France, and Spaniards just back from Russian training schools. It was a kind of foreign legion of the air, and the comradeship among the pilots was much like that of the old Western Front days. However, Bell quickly learned that chivalry in the air had been buried at the same time the Armistice was signed. "So far," Bell said, "it had been a nice war." Then Bell and the others flew their first combat patrol near Madrid.

Bell, because of his World War I experience, was placed above and behind the rest of the squadron to act as rear protection. The squadron was led by an aggressive, but inexperienced Spanish pilot who fell for one of the original "sucker traps" dating back to 1917. Bell recalled that they were at 12,000 feet in the bright blue winter sky when he spotted twenty Italian Fiats in formation 4,000 feet further down. Instinctively, Bell put his thumb against the sun's disk and, as he had guessed, there were other planes lurking above. But Bell's squadron leader recklessly dived for the enemy below and the trap was sprung.

In the wild melee that followed, Bell shot down one of the Fiats before the fight was a minute old. He was shocked; it had been nearly twenty years since he had seen combat and he had forgotten what war was like. "The converging fire of four guns slammed him as if he had been hit by a truck. He went straight down and I was behind him. The pilot's head turned slightly, sun-glint on the goggles. Then, in a most agonizing movement, he put his hands behind his head as though to ward off the bullets. His Fiat went down in a tight spin and never came out of it. This was no game. I saw this man die. I saw his helmet turn from black to strawberry red. I saw him fall against his instrument panel."

Momentarily stunned at what had happened—at what he had made happen—Bell flew on as though in a dream, not thinking to look behind. The Heinkel fighters that had been upsun fell upon the Loyalist planes in a fury. They reminded Bell of "skittering silver fish, filling the air with a thousand javelins of tracer fire." Bell was hit almost immediately; a machine-gun slug

3

ripped through his helmet, gouging a furrow of flesh in his right temple. The blow knocked Bell unconscious, his hands and feet relaxed at the controls and the fighter whipped into a tight spin. Two Heinkel pilots followed Bell's whirling plane all the way down to a thousand feet above the ground, firing steadily, trying to make sure of a victim. Bell came to, saw the earth rushing toward him, and got his feet on the rudder bars and worked them in harmony with the stick and pulled the nose up. He had come out of the spin directly over a zigzag line of Nationalist trenches and the troops below were firing at him with rifles and machine guns. Bullets zipped past the cockpit and Bell climbed away. The Heinkels were gone. Despite the terrific pain in his head, despite the blood seeping into his right eye, temporarily blinding him, despite his recent fright, all Bell could think about was striking back. He banked the fighter around and came down on the deck strafing the Nationalist trenches with his four machine guns. One gun jammed, but the others kept firing. "The soldiers scattered and fell like ninepins—not human beings to me, but toy soldiers such as you knock over with rubber cannon balls on the playroom floor." Bell kept firing until the ammunition was gone, then turned for the base near Madrid, where the doctor treated the wound by pouring raw iodine into the furrow and marking him fit for duty.

The dogfight had gone in favor of the Loyalists. Fourteen of the enemy had been shot down; three of the Loyalist pilots had been killed; Tex Allison limped home with a gaping wound in his leg from an illegal mushroom bullet, and Whitey Dahl had been shot down behind the Fascist lines. Instead of being "binged" by the enemy pilots, Dahl was thrown into a dirty cell and told he would soon face a firing squad. Only intervention by an American officer who had fought with Franco in Morocco saved Dahl's life.

This first heavy engagement proved that the war in the air was going to be as tough as the war on the ground, but what happened a few days later shocked pilots who believed themselves unshockable. During another bitter clash with the Nationalists, a young Spanish Loyalist pilot named Luis Muñoz shot down an enemy fighter and watched the pilot bail out from the crippled plane. When the chute popped Muñoz bored in and machine-gunned the Nationalist pilot swaying helplessly in the risers. Revenge was swift. One of the Loyalist pilots was forced down behind the Fascist lines not long afterwards. He returned to his friends in a gruesome way: a Heinkel bomber flew over Bell's field one bright morning and dropped a large box at the end of a parachute. Inside were the dismembered remains of the captured Loyalist, and pinned to one of the pieces were scribbled insults written in Italian. Bell went behind a hangar and was "good and sick."

Clearly, this was not a war for gentlemen.

Shrecklichkeit is a German word that means "frightfulness," and it was a word much in use inside the war-planning rooms of the OKW, the German High Command, when the groundwork was being laid for World War II. The idea was brutally simple: make war so frightful that the enemy's will to resist would be broken early in the game. Smash his cities, terrorize the civilian population, thus demoralizing the fighting men. The generals at OKW decided to put theory into practice somewhere in Spain. The tools—bombers and fighters of the Condor Legion; the target—a small town named Guernica, not far from the northern Spanish coast. Guernica was a famous old Basque town of almost no military importance. The majority of the town's 7,000 inhabitants were strongly anti-fascist. Farmers came to Guernica every Monday to sell vegetables and to gossip in the town square, and it was on Monday, April 26, 1937, that the unsuspecting people of Guernica had their taste of frightfulness.

It was a little after 4:30 in the afternoon when the church bells began to toll the warning. Looking into the sky, the people crowded inside the square saw late afternoon sunlight glinting from the silver wings of a wave of Heinkel 111 twin-engined bombers. Above them, a flawless formation of

German Arado 195, seen here on floats, was used by Franco fliers as reconnaissance craft.

Heinkel 51 fighters. They were low, and those with keen eyes could see the bomb-bay doors of the 111s swing open. Some of the people stood rooted where they were, others fled up the streets. The first bombs fell. Concussion waves swept people off their feet and shattered windows. Half-ton iron-and-high-explosive bombs plunged through roofs to explode deep inside, scattering splintered wood and chunks of stone for hundreds of yards in every direction. Hundreds of incendiary missiles were sown haphazardly and Guernica was ablaze. When the first wave of bombers wheeled homeward to reload with deadly cargoes, the fighters swept in and machine-gunned the streets. Men, women, and children were killed as they ran.

With Teutonic precision, fresh waves of bombers flew back and forth over the stricken town every twenty minutes until dusk obscured the scene of horror. Three hours of merciless bombing and strafing left more than 1,600 killed and 900 wounded.

What did Guernica prove? Simply this: small, undefended towns could be virtually destroyed, given enough time and enough bombs. The policy of frightfulness was not vindicated, however. The troops occupying the Loyalist trenches, instead of becoming demoralized, were rededicated. The world was shocked, and those whose sympathies had been uncertain now turned toward the Loyalists. In London, Fighter Command heeded the lesson

Sleek Heinkel 51 fighters were used as escorts for He–111s, which nearly obliterated the little Basque town of Guernica.

and had second thoughts about beefing up interceptor defenses throughout the British Isles.

Later in the war, the Italians staged a five-hour shuttle of bombers over the great city of Barcelona and killed more than 1,300 civilians. Again, the rest of the world was stunned, but dictator Benito Mussolini—who had ordered the bombing—said that he was "delighted that the Italians should be horrifying the world by their aggressiveness for a change instead of charming it by the guitar." As it turned out, Mussolini wished many times that he had stayed with music instead of bombs.

Because the Nationalists were outnumbered in fighter strength, the German pilots of the Condor Legion had their own way with a new tactical terror weapon introduced during the latter stages of the Spanish Civil War. That weapon was the Junkers 87 dive bomber. The Ju–87 was one of the ugliest airplanes ever built, but it did a good job in Spain and earned an infamous reputation there and in the early stages of World War II. Powered by a Junkers Jumo 635-hp in-line engine, the Ju–87A–1 "Stuka," as it was called, was capable of only 199 mph and was armed with but one 7.9-mm machine gun firing forward and another on a swivel mount firing aft. The Stuka's "big gun" was the 550-pound bomb slung underneath the fuselage, attached to a metal strut shaped like a crutch. Stukas bombed by diving vertically at pinpoint targets. The strut holding the bomb was extended so that the missile would clear the arc of the propeller. If the mission called for it, the Stuka's observer-gunner could be left on the ground so that an 1,100-pound bomb could be carried.

Masterminding the use of air power by the Condor Legion was its Chief of Staff, Wolfram von Richthofen, youngest brother of Manfred, Germany's greatest fighter ace of World War I. As von Richthofen saw it, air power's greatest usefulness lay in operations that supported the infantry, directly and indirectly. He used the Stukas to bomb harbors and ships, which denied Loyalist infantry needed tools of war, and he used them on the battlefields to bomb strong points, observation posts, machine gun nests, and tanks. Stuka pilots seldom pulled out of dives above 3,000 feet and could place their big bombs within twenty or thirty feet of the target. Loyalist troops often found to their dismay that desperately needed bridges had been blown by Stukas only minutes before they arrived to cross some deep gorge, frustrating carefully laid attack plans.

Stuka, carrying Nationalist markings, but flown by German volunteer, returns from dive-bombing mission somewhere in Spain.

When attacking large targets, von Richthofen sent his planes over in layers. The He–111s went in low, carpeting the target with bombs. Above were the vital fighters, usually no fewer than twenty in number, whose job was seeing that no audacious Loyalist pilots could penetrate the defensive screen in order to get at the bombers. Strung out along the edge of the armada were the Stukas, waiting to pounce on the earth when the Heinkels' bomb bays were emptied. With the Heinkels out of the way, the Stukas formed up line astern like some great serpent and peeled off one after another to deliver their own loads of destruction with unerring accuracy. This angular ugly gull-wing shape screamed like a banshee as it hurtled toward the ground at 350 mph, and troops on the ground hated them worse than any any other airplane.

With the introduction into combat of the Me–109B fighter, the Loyalist pilots in their stubby little I–16s stood little chance in the same sky. The Me–109B with its 670-hp Jumo engine could touch 300 mph and carried three machine guns. The worth of this new fighter was proved by one of the young Condor Legion pilots named Werner Molders, twenty-five, who flew Willi Messerschmitt's creation during the final months of the war and shot down fourteen Loyalist airplanes, more than any other fighter pilot during the conflict.

The Spanish Civil War ended in March 1939, with total victory for Francisco Franco's Nationalists. The foreigners went home, taking with them the fruits of their experience. The Germans learned more than anybody else. They proved that mass air attacks could pulverize and terrorize small towns. They tested and improved tactical methods for dive bombers and fighters to pave the way for infantry ground assaults. They discovered that their new Me–109 was better than anything other nations committed to combat in Spanish skies. The Germans came away bloodied, experienced, and filled with new knowledge. But, as events would prove, they had not learned enough.

Confident, arrogant, they prepared to plunge the world into the greatest war in history.

Brave Poles flew monoplane P-6 fighters against Luftwaffe Me–109s and 111s in one hopeless battle after another when Germans invaded Poland in 1939.

2/FIGHTERS NORTH

WHILE THE CIVIL WAR in Spain was running its course, momentous events were taking place in the rest of Europe. Adolf Hitler, absolute dictator of Nazi Germany, had committed the Third Reich to a policy of conquest. The Rhineland, Austria, the Sudetenland, then all of Czechoslovakia were literally annexed; all fell without bloodshed. Then, on September 1, 1939, the German panzers struck across the Polish frontier. The Poles, fiercely proud of their independence, fought back, and World War II was ushered into the pages of history.

Techniques used in Spain were employed against Poland. Waves of He–111s and Dornier 17 bombers escorted by twin-engine Messerschmitt 110 fighters battered their way through handfuls of Polish fighters to unload tons of high explosive bombs on the city of Warsaw. Stukas howled down out of the sky to smash bridges and tanks and armored cars. The Polish Fighter Brigade was equipped largely with P–7 single-seat fighters, graceful gull-wing monoplanes with radial engines that were no match for the Me–109s. But the Poles flung themselves against the Germans with desperate courage, occasionally bringing down German bombers before they became victims themselves of superior equipment thrown against them in greater numbers.

One of the survivors of the ruthless aerial campaign waged in Polish skies, a fighter pilot named Witold Urbanowicz, describes what it was like:

"The sky was full of German planes. Colonel Pamula shot down two bombers, then his ammunition ran out and he was attacked by two Me–109s. He steered straight for one of the enemy fighters, then bailed out only seconds before the impact. On the first day we of the Fighter Brigade lost ten aircraft destroyed and another twenty-four were so badly shot up they were out of action. The Brigade was down to twenty fighters ready for combat the

11

next day. Mechanics and pilots worked through the night to repair the battle-damaged P–7s, managing to patch twenty of them by the next night.

"By September 6, the Front had gone all to pieces, and we were down to only twenty-one fighters, most of which were kept flying by some miracle. With this deplorable equipment we went up to do battle with several dozen German bombers with fighter cover. We broke up the German formations in a battle lasting over an hour, withdrawing from the fight only when out of fuel. Our attacks were so furious that in this mad frenzy two German bombers crashed into each other and exploded. Not a single German bomber broke through to Warsaw. The Brigade that day shot down twelve of the enemy, and the pilots were so afire with the heat of battle that, returning on the last drops of fuel and many with no ammunition, they pounced on thirty Stukas they met on their way, scattering them in all directions. But we paid the price of three planes and pilots, none of whom could be replaced.

"By September 8, there were only sixteen planes left to us and we were forced to move our operational base further and further back as the panzers ground forward. We flew lacking sleep and often without food. The fuel situation was so tragic that air patrols were sent out to find tank cars on railway lines; then, after checking whether or not they actually contained fuel, trucks were sent out to bring the precious gasoline back in barrels. But the trucks could not keep pace with the planes, held up as they were by the increasing chaos on the roads, which were constantly under attack from the air."

A week later, the Polish Fighter Brigade was totally out of fuel, there was nothing for the achingly tired pilots and mechanics to eat, and all communications with other units were severed. Enough gasoline was scrounged to make possible a few flights on September 17, when the Brigade bagged its final German bomber. It was all over. Poland, a nation nearly the size of Texas, was crushed within two weeks in the first demonstration of Hitler's *Blitzkrieg,* lightning war pressed with relentless speed using armor, motorized infantry, and, above all, powerful air support. The *Luftwaffe* seemed invincible.

France and the British Empire declared war on Germany immediately after the fighting began in Poland, and the world waited for the clash of great armies along the Western Front. The people of London, with the horrors of the bombing of Warsaw fresh in mind, steeled themselves for the onslaught of the Luftwaffe. But the expected trial by fire hung in suspension. Looking backward to the First World War, the French assumed a defensive attitude and buried themselves deep in the concrete bowels of the Maginot Line, and the Germans seemed content to rest after their labors in Poland. Through the fall and early spring of 1940 the world witnessed an uneasy interlude that became known as "The Phony War," and wondered what would happen next.

Far to the north, new and unexpected events leapt into the headlines. Mammoth Russia was pressuring its tiny neighbor, Finland, demanding a gift of strategic territory on the Karelian Isthmus where the two nations joined. The Finns—tough, proud, and fiercely independent—were overwhelmingly outnumbered in every way; the Russians could send more than 800 aircraft against Finland, but the Finns had only 100 planes of all kinds to resist an invasion. The Finns were short of everything except raw courage and skill. If you want our land, they said, come and take it. Those unfamiliar with Finnish character and hardihood said that the Finnish defiance was like a rabbit challenging a bear.

On the morning of November 30, 1939, a senior Finnish flying officer, Colonel Riku Lorentz, dashed into the command post of a Finnish forward fighter squadron base and fired a pistol shot through the ceiling. The startled pilots looked up in astonishment as the graying colonel announced that the nation was at war, that Russian forces were crossing the frontier in force, that Red bombers were already penetrating Finnish skies. The pilots grabbed up their helmets and ran outside to their waiting fighters. Five minutes later the squadron was airborne in the wintry air, headed for the old fortress town of Viipuri. The pilots, flying their first combat sortie, were tense with excite-

Finns flew Dutch-built Fokker D–21 fighters against Russians in opening phase of the "Winter War."

ment. Would they reach Viipuri in time? Would their opponents be skilled veterans of the Spanish Civil War, or were they peacetime fighter pilots like themselves? How many Russians would they find? Would the weather hold? They were already down to 2,000 feet, just under a dirty base of cloud that seemed to drop lower with every passing minute. The long hand on the panel clock dragged by. Twenty mintues after takeoff the Finnish fighters were over Viipuri. Black smoke boiled up from the earth; the Russians had come and gone, dropping their bombs on the railroad yards. The Finns climbed up through the clouds to seek the enemy. They broke through into a dazzling world of sunshine and azure skies, but there was no sign of the enemy. They patrolled for an hour, sweeping back and forth, but the Russians did not come back that day, and the Finns, their excitement siphoned off by disappointment, flew back home through worsening weather. It began to snow, gently at first, then with a frenzy whipped by bitter winds. The fighters were landed in a dark gray gloom; it was only eleven in the morning, but the sun was blotted from view. Hurrying through the snowstorm the pilots sought the warmth of their huts, there to contemplate the future of the Winter War.

On hand to combat the Russians were thirty-one near-obsolete Fokker D.XXI fighters, a low-wing, fixed-gear, metal-plywood-and-fabric aircraft that was phased into service with the Finnish Air Force in 1938. The plane was designed by the Dutch genius of World War I, Anthony Fokker, and was characteristically Fokker in its clean lines and light weight, grossing out on takeoff at only 4,519 pounds. The range of the Fokker D.XXI was 590 miles at normal cruise speed of 215 mph, sufficient for the role the airplane would play in the limited area over which the air war would be fought. Powered with a 725-hp Mercury radial air-cooled engine, the D.XXI's top speed was 285 mph and the maximum ceiling topped out at just over 31,000 feet— speeds and altitudes sufficient to cope with the Russian bombers used early in the war. Armament was adequate to deal with most Russian planes of earlier vintage, consisting of four Browning 7.9-mm (.30-caliber) machine guns. The little fighter was maneuverable in the air, but required finesse when landing, a fact pilots fresh from training schools learned to their sorrow. Finns looked upon this Fokker with affection, although they wished it were faster and that there were more of them.

The Finns adopted the only defensive tactics available to them, considering the pitiful number of fighters operational. Each squadron kept two fighters

14

aloft over designated areas ninety minutes at a time, while the remainder of the pilots stood by in ready rooms, waiting for flashes from the alert tent that large formations of Russian bombers were on the way. It was during one of these round-robin patrols on the second day of the war that the Finns claimed their first victory.

Captain Eino Luukaanen and his wingman intercepted a pair of Russian SB–2 twin-engined bombers flying at 3,000 feet just below Lake Ladoga, bound on some mission of destruction. Luukaanen was a veteran pilot, but this was his first combat. He hurled his fighter directly at the enemy bomber, closing the range until he was less than 100 yards from the rear of the SB–2. He opened fire at the same time as the Russian gunner and watched as "brilliant orange flashes danced in front of my windscreen." The Finn was so intent on bagging the big Russian bomber that he nearly rammed it. He banked sharply away and turned and once again got on the Russian's tail. He and the Russian gunner traded fire, but neither scored crippling strikes. The Russian pilot jettisoned his bombs, and by this time was so close to the ground that the concussion tossed Luukaanen's fighter like paper in a stiff breeze. The Finn got control of the Fokker and bored in for the third time. The Russian dropped his landing gear, slowing the bomber, and the Fokker overshot, giving the Russian front gunner a crack at him. Luukaanen banked around and cut back on the throttle, slowing his own attack speed. He flew into Russian guns until he was only fifty yards away, then poured a long burst of fire into the Russian's wing. One engine belched black smoke, then the propeller flicked to a stop. The Russian bomber was now less than 100 feet from the ground, so the pilot put the SB–2 down in the nearest field.

Luukaanen flashed overhead and saw that the three crewmen had climbed

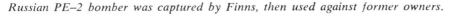

Russian PE–2 bomber was captured by Finns, then used against former owners.

out and were waving white pieces of cloth at him as a sign of surrender. Elated, Luukaanen had a wild idea: why not land beside the downed bomber and personally take the Russians captive? Then, "realizing what a damned fool idea it was," he poured the gas to his fighter and flew back home. The other members of his squadron were so elated that they picked up the victorious pilot and tossed him up and down in the air as though he were a child.

As winter deepened the cold grew almost unbearable. In January 1940, temperatures plunged to twenty and thirty degrees below zero and stayed there. The Finnish pilots muffled themselves to the ears in fur and donned high felt boots over several pairs of socks, and still they froze. The Fokkers could not be hangared, but instead were left dispersed around the forward flying fields covered only with white canvas. It often took as long as half an hour to warm the oil and hydraulic fluids sufficiently so that the engines would develop maximum revs, so that the guns could fire. For days on end there was no flying because of heavy and continuous snowfall. It was the worst winter ever recorded in Finland, and nobody suffered as much as did the Russian troops trying to batter their way through the frozen swamps and dark forests the Finns fought so desperately to hold. The Russians, surprisingly, were not as well protected against the deadly cold as were the Finns, who were warmly dressed and provided with white camouflage capes that made them almost invisible against the endless stretches of snow that covered all of Finland. Ski patrols struck the miserable Russian troops at unexpected places and there was dark slaughter with guns, knives, and fists. Russian soldiers, conspicuous in their brown uniforms, froze in grotesque positions and did not thaw until the spring.

Once the Finnish fighter squadrons were sent after a battalion of the Red Army trying to cross a frozen lake, seeking to flank Finnish positions in the north of Karelia. The weather there was in the clear, but fog and clouds obscured the Russian fighter base a few miles away so that the Fokkers were unhindered in their work. There were about 500 Russians struggling across the ice, urging forward horse-drawn wagons and light artillery. The Finns caught them completely by surprise. The Fokkers got right down on the deck, less than fifty feet above the lake, and lined up in single file to rake the Russians again and again. There was no place to hide, and the Russians slipped and scurried this way and that trying to avoid the thirty-two machine guns that hammered at them until every round of ammunition had been ex-

16

pended. The survivors crawled back from the frozen lake, totally defeated by the fighters.

The Russians began sending over bomber swarms in larger numbers, usually no fewer than two dozen at a time. They were escorted by the stubby Russian I–16 Mosca (Fly) fighters that had been tested in Spain. Life for the Finnish pilots, who were being killed one by one, was a blur of taking off, landing to refuel and rearm, taking off again to fight, landing, taking off, dying, being wounded, staying cold to the bone, always hungry, always fatigued. Fokkers were being lost that could not be replaced. The British managed to deliver a handful of Gloster Gladiator biplanes to the Finnish Fighter Command, and these slow, poorly armed machines joined with the sleeker Fokkers to battle the Russians.

On February 28, this mixed bag of Finnish interceptors took off to engage a Russian aerial armada of twenty-one bombers and thirty-six Russian-built Moscas and I–153 fighter biplanes. Fifteen D.XXIs and Gladiators had barely gotten off the field when the Russians jumped them. The Finns had to fight their way through the swarm while still climbing for effective combat altitude. They noticed that the Russian fighters were painted in gaudy colors. The ensuing melee was something that had not been seen in the air since the wildest of the 1918-era dogfights. Individual combats swirled from treetop level to a mile above the earth. Planes plunged for the ground trailing smoke and flames. Others disintegrated in midair. The sky blossomed with parachutes, the air filled with the crackling of machine guns and the snarl of engines. In fifteen minutes, it was all over. One of the Fokkers and five of the old Gladiators had been shot down. One of the Finns died when he deliberately rammed another Russian fighter. Eight Russian planes had been knocked down, but the bombers got through and bombed their targets.

The unbelievable stand the Finns were making against the Russian giant stirred the sympathy of most of the world. Three nations still neutral—the United States, Norway, and Sweden—decided to help. The United States declared surplus forty-five Brewster B–239 Buffalo fighters and released them for use by the Finns. The Buffalo had been designed as a shipboard fighter for the U.S. Navy and was more advanced than anything either the Finns or the Russians had operational at the time. The Buffalo looked like a flying barrel. Powered with a 950-hp radial engine, the fighter could top 300 mph, climbed at better than 3,000 feet per minute, and had an unusually long range of more than 1,000 miles. It carried four .50-caliber machine guns that could blast

17

Skis enable Finns to fly from frozen lakes or snow-covered fields, but open cockpit of captured Russian I–16 made flying a test of endurance.

through Russian armor plate and ruin even the best of Russian self-sealing fuel tanks. To the beleagured Finns, such a quantity of new fighters meant life or death in the skies.

The first batch of Brewsters were sent to Trollhatten, Sweden, where the Swedes would help with the flight test program. Volunteer Norwegian mechanics and fitters went to Sweden to work on the new planes, and an American naval pilot, Lieutenant Robert A. Winston, volunteered to teach Finnish pilots how to master the Buffalo when they were delivered to the fighting zone. Winston found the Finns eager students and quick learners. He was so enthusiastic that he planned to fly against the Russians himself in one of the chunky fighters after all of the Finns had been checked out. There is no doubt that the Buffalos would have made a tremendous difference in the Winter War in the air, but only three were delivered before the Red Army overran all of Karelia, when the Finns negotiated an armistice on March 13. The struggle against the Russians lasted 105 days, days that the world will never forget. The Finns burned or blew up every building in the slow, bitter pullback, leaving the Russians only scorched earth and the frozen corpses of their dead. To the Finns, the war was not yet decided; there was only an armistice.*

On April 9, 1940, the Phony War in Europe exploded with the sudden

*On June 22, 1941, the Germans launched a massive attack against the Soviet Union. A day later the Russians again attacked the Finns and the war was on again. The Finns recaptured all of the land lost in the Winter War, fighting as stubbornly as before. Eino Luukaanen, flying Buffalos and Me–109Gs, shot down 48 more Russian planes to raise his total of kills to 51.

Russian L–15 fighters, taken intact, warming up to be flown by Finnish pilots somewhere in Karelia.

blitzkrieg against Denmark and Norway. The Germans quickly overran neighboring Danish soil, but against the Norwegians they had tougher going. Norway had been neutral during World War I and had seen no cause to spend its scanty funds on a large national defense force during the following years. In fact, the Norwegians took in thousands of orphaned and starving German children in 1919 and fed and clothed them as though they were their own. Now many of these same Germans were back as paratroopers and seaborne invaders.

To meet the enemy in the air, the Royal Norwegian Air Force was equipped with nine Gloster Gladiator biplanes, a design that had first flown in England in 1934. The fighter was powered with a nine-cylinder air-cooled radial Bristol Mercury engine that gave the aircraft a maximum speed of 245 mph at 15,000 feet. There were four .303 Browning machine guns, two firing through the propeller and two mounted in streamlined pods underneath the wings. The plane reached its operational ceiling at just above 32,000 feet, had a range of 400 miles, and could climb to 10,000 feet in a little over four minutes. Thus, for the late 1930s, the Gladiator was a handy little interceptor—but this was 1940 and the Germans were flying Me–109s, not Fokker triplanes. Of the nine Gladiators of the Norwegian Fighter Wing based at Fornebu airport, near Oslo, only seven were operational; the other two were grounded for lack of spark plugs.

At 0700 on April 9, the Norwegians hurled their entire fighter force against the invading German Luftwaffe. The primary target was the capital city, Oslo, and the largest airfield in the nation, Fornebu. The Germans had no wish to give these targets the same treatment they gave Warsaw; they hoped that the Norwegians would accept the protection they, the Luftwaffe and the Wehrmacht, offered from the British! To the strange German mind Norwegians were almost as good as the Germans because, ethnically, they were related in a Nordic strain. Plan Weser, Hitler's code name for the invasion of Denmark and Norway, envisioned a lightning seizure of both countries using simultaneous strikes by paratroopers and marine landings at strategic points so there would be no time to organize resistance. If resistance was encountered, then the bombers that were sent to accompany the troop-carrying Ju–52s could give the Norwegians a taste of frightfulness.

So it was when the five Gladiators climbed up to greet the Luftwaffe they found the sky approaches to Oslo alive with enemy aircraft. Leading the Norwegian fighters was Lieutenant Rolf Tradin, whose heart sank when he looked down the snow-spotted fjord at the approaching German armada. He had never seen so many airplanes at one time in his entire life. There were He–111s, Dornier 17s, twin-engined Me–110 fighters, and lumbering Ju–52s. He started counting, reached a count of seventy, then stopped. What was the use? There were at least twice that many. He led the tiny formation to 5,500 feet, then dived into the swarm of black-crossed planes moving serenely along 2,000 feet below. He picked an He–111 and waded in from above and to the rear, riddling the bomber's right wing and setting ablaze the starboard engine. The bomber banked to the right then drunkenly rolled over and began an inverted spiral toward the cold deep waters of the Oslofjord. There was no time to watch the final agonies of the German crew; Tradin was in the middle of the bomber stream, snapshooting at targets all around him. He weaved his way in and out of the roaring melee, through a

American Brewster F2A Buffalo was assembled in Sweden, flown to Finland for use against Russians late in the war.

Hardy Finns and Norwegians flew Gloster Gladiator biplane fighters against Russian and German aircraft, and almost always against hopeless odds.

web of German tracer bullets until his guns overheated and jammed. Then he dived for home. As he banked in and straightened out for final approach the radio crackled in his ears. It was the CO, Captain Erling Dahl, down in the operations shack. "All Gladiators. Fornebu under attack by German bombers. Land elsewhere." Tradin hiked the nose of his biplane up and hurtled past an He–111 unloading bombs. He flew on to land on the thick ice of a deep fjord north of Oslo.

Following Tradin into combat, Sergeant Per Waaler shot down one HE–111, kept attacking until his guns were empty, then landed at Fornebu with a dead engine. He had time only to get out of the cockpit and dive for a foxhole before an Me–110 roared overhead on a strafing pass. When Waaler looked up he saw that his own Gladiator and one other parked nearby were blazing brightly.

Sergeant Per Schye crippled a Dornier 17, watched it crash-land in the snow north of the city. Schye climbed and made a firing pass at two Heinkels, but a third bomber was behind him and the German gunner shot the Gladiator full of holes. The Norwegian pilot watched his instrument panel disintegrate, then felt a hammerblow and his left arm go numb. Blood seeped down his sleeve and was whipped into a fine red spray from the wind blowing through the holes in the cockpit. He spiraled toward the earth, managed to level out over a patch of clean ground. He saw the high voltage wire stretched before him too late to get the nose up. The Gladiator struck the wire and somersaulted into the ground. Miraculously. Schye was able to crawl from the wreckage and walk to a farmhouse, where he collapsed and was driven to a hospital.

21

Another pilot in Tradin's flight, Lieutenant Dag Krohn, survived to give his own account of the battle against the German bombers. "I managed to shoot down an He–111 and a Do–17. I was jumped by a pair of Me–110s and managed to lose them by flying into the clouds. I climbed out on top and immediately attacked another German aircraft flying below. I killed the tail gunner and got in good strikes elsewhere, but I lost the German in the clouds. I heard Captain Dahl's order not to land at Fornebu before the radio fell silent. I returned to Fornebu anyway and saw that some Ju–52s had already landed. I flew down and strafed some others that were on the point of landing; then I flew off to find some place to land myself.

"I landed on the northeastern bay of Tyrifjord, where I found Lieutenant Tradin who had set down there only a few minutes before."

Tradin and Krohn managed to take off from the ice and flew northward to Hamar, where they landed on a frozen lake. Tradin's wheels sank through to the fuselage and had to be abandoned. Krohn's oil reservoir was drained and the oil transferred to a Caproni bomber. There was no more oil for the fighter there, so the Gladiator was towed to cover and abandoned.

Lieutenant Arve Braaten took off from Fornebu with a faltering engine, but managed to climb to combat altitude and duel with a pair of German bombers. His ammunition exhausted, the engine running rough, Braaten broke off combat and he, too, landed on a partially frozen lake. The wheels punched through the ice and the Gladiator stuck fast. Braaten climbed out of the fighter and never saw it again.

Thus within less than two hours the entire Norwegian Fighter Wing was used up in combat. The Germans paid a price above the one they had rendered in the air; Norwegian ground gunners shot down eight Ju–52 transports and seven Me–110s over the airfield, while another four of the twin-engined fighters went down on the outskirts of Oslo. The Germans had not expected such stiff resistance, and more was to come.

While the German mountain troops were fighting their way north, down into the valleys and across seemingly endless rugged mountain ranges still blanketed with snow, help was on the way for the scattered bands of Norwegian troops who contested every foot of ground. On April 15, 17, and 18, the Allies landed at three separate points along the western coast of Norway. The units included some of the most famous regimental names in British history, plus a Polish brigade and experienced French troops of the Chasseurs

Alpins and the Foreign Legion. The reinforcements ran into trouble almost immediately; the Germans had firm command of the air and bombed and strafed at will. The hard-pressed ground commanders called for air support.

On April 24, the British aircraft carrier *Glorious* entered Norwegian waters and launched eighteen Gladiators of No. 263 Squadron. The biplanes landed on the frozen surface of Lake Lesjaskog, seventy-five miles inland, 250 miles north of Oslo, and prepared to do battle with the Germans. Conditions could not have been worse for the British pilots and ground crew. The lake was 2,000 feet above sea level and the thermometer registered only two degrees above zero. The planes, parked in the open, quickly froze; the controls were locked solid and the carburetors were blocks of ice. The ground crews were short-handed; for instance, there was but one trained armorer to service the seventy-two machine guns on the Gladiators.

The pilots and mechanics were up before dawn, stamping their feet to get the circulation going and drinking mugs of hot tea in a vain attempt to warm themselves. Shortage of equipment coupled with the intense cold delayed the takeoff of the first Gladiator for more than two hours to oppose the waves of German bombers that started a day-long attack on the frozen lake. A few He–111s were shot down, but more came, dumping bombs everywhere. Gaping holes were torn in the ice, and fighter planes, struck by 500-pound bombs, were blown to bits. The lake was guarded by only a pair of 20-mm quick-firing cannon and a few Lewis guns, and ammunition for these was soon exhausted. The few Gladiators that managed to get into the air fought the Germans until not one round of belted .303 ammunition was left, then they landed on the cratered surface of the lake, still under bombardment. With thirteen of the fighters lying smashed on the ice, the lake was abandoned and the five remaining Gladiators were flown to another field. But by the afternoon of the next day, only one was left.

The survivors of No. 263 Squadron, led by Squadron Leader "Baldy" Donaldson, returned to England on a merchant ship and were assigned a new batch of planes. These Gladiators, plus No. 46 Squadron, equipped with the far more powerful Hawker Hurricanes, were loaded aboard the carrier H.M.S. *Furious* and sent to fly from the airfield at Bardufoss, far above the Arctic Circle. The pilots knew how badly they were needed; the outnumbered British, Norwegian, French, and Polish riflemen holding out against the relentless German advance lay crouched in ditches along the approaches to Trondheim, cringing at the angry snarl of Stukas that ranged

The Allies grew to hate the deadly silhouette of the He–111, never a handsome airplane to begin with.

at will, bombing and machine-gunning everything that moved. A British brigadier named Dudley Clarke told how it was:

"The German pilots flew just as they liked, up and down that one narrow road along which everything had to move. With their bombs spent they would drop down on their remaining petrol for the sport of shooting up everything in sight. That first attack either got you or missed you; and then, after it was over, there would follow the exhausting process of tumbling out and ploughing through snow to the nearest tree or wall, or even the roadside drain, in the few minutes that were left for the next one. . . ."

Brigadier Clarke summed up the feelings of the infantryman under air attack when he said, "Looking back upon it, I believe the 'Evil Eye' feeling was the worst part, the sensation of being watched at every turn by birds of prey who could swoop with deadly suddenness whenever they chose the moment."

It was German air power that rendered the Allied ground forces all but immobilized during the fifteen hours of daylight offered by the Norwegian spring.

The Gladiators and the Hurricanes flown from the field at Bardufoss delivered stinging blows to the Luftwaffe, but the Allied campaign in Norway was doomed from the start; there were simply too many Germans too well organized. On May 25, it was decided to evacuate the country, leaving the Norwegians to their fate. It was a hard decision for Britain's Prime Minister, Winston Churchill, to have to make, but every British soldier, truck, rifle, and airplane would be needed for the further trials ahead. The

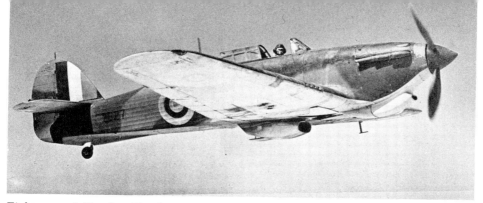

Eight-gunned Hawker Hurricane was no match for Germany's faster Messerschmitt, which could outclimb and outdive the British fighter.

Gladiators and Hurricanes provided the air cover vitally needed for the British ships to take aboard the Allied troops, then were ordered to leave Bardufoss and fly back to H.M.S. *Glorious* for transportation back to England.

It was one thing for the lighter, slower Gladiators to fly aboard the narrow, shifting flight deck of an aircraft carrier, but quite another for the heavier, faster Hurricanes that were designed to be operated from long and wide concrete runways. At first, the Hurricanes of No. 46 Squadron were ordered demolished, but 46's commander, Squadron Leader "Bing" Cross, loudly protested the destruction of the Hurricanes, pointing out that every fighter plane would be sorely needed in the days to come. Britain had few enough fighters as it was. He all but demanded permission for his pilots to attempt the hazardous carrier landing, and it was given.

Ten surviving Gladiators and eight surviving Hurricanes were guided to the *Glorious* by a Royal Navy Swordfish. The Gladiators, as expected, put down with no trouble; then everybody watched as the Hurricanes made their approach. They came in at minimum speed, with full flaps, and pitched up at a higher than normal angle of attack; they were flying just above the threshold of a full stall when they came in, and this was how the eight precious fighters were brought safely down.

But, as so often in war, great gallantry and skill went for nothing. On the afternoon of June 8, while the *Glorious* was steaming for England, she was caught by the German "pocket battleship" *Gneisenau* and was hit again and again by the 11-inch shells fired from long range. The carrier was turned into a mass of flames, and in the early afternoon, badly listing, she sank. Nearly 1,500 men died with the *Glorious* under the dark, freezing waters of the North Sea. Only forty-six crewmen survived.

The airpower disaster was complete.

This Hurricane II, fitted with four 20-mm cannons, was capable of crippling German fighters or bombers with only a few strikes.

3/THIN RED LINE

EVEN AS THE GERMANS were mopping up in Norway, they unleashed a tidal wave of tanks and airpower against Belgium, Holland, and France. The smaller nations were quickly overrun, and the world was stunned when the French collapsed after only six weeks of fighting; the Germans simply bypassed the famed Maginot Line, plunging through the dense Ardennes forest and across the rolling plains of the Somme in a concentration of armor that the French were powerless to stop. On June 21, 1940, the French signed an armistice at Compiègne, Hitler danced a jig for Wehrmacht photographers, and now England stood alone.

All that stood between the British people and total subjugation was a handful of youthful fighter pilots of the Royal Air Force. Prime Minister Winston Churchill put the blunt truth to his people in a radio address on the evening of June 18. "I expect that the Battle of Britain is about to begin," he warned. "The whole fury and might of the enemy must very soon be turned on us. Hitler knows that he must break us in this island or lose the war. Let us therefore brace ourselves to our duties," he growled, "and so bear ourselves that, if the British Empire and its Commonwealth last for a thousand years, men will say, 'This was their finest hour.' "

Across the English Channel, only twenty-two miles wide at its narrowest point, the Germans, flushed with victory and eager to get at England and end the war, were bombarded with propaganda from loudspeakers blaring from nearly every corner. A special song had even been written in Berlin in anticipation of the coming battle. It was called *"Bomben Auf Engeland"* and as a youthful German general named Adolf Galland recalled, the song was played "on all the loudspeakers from Aachen to Tilsit, from Flensburg to Innsbruck, and from most of the army stations in the occupied countries. But," said Galland, "we pilots could not stand this song from the very start."

27

These cannon-carrying Spitfires are seen in modified finger-four formation, which proved superior to all other formations when attacking Luftwaffe bomber streams or fighter escorts.

Galland knew, if the German Propaganda Ministry did not, that the Luftwaffe would get its bombs on England only at heavy sacrifice.

The Germans opened the battle with more than 2,000 fighters and bombers. Operationally deployed were 860 twin-engined bombers, 650 Me–109s, 200 Me–110s, 250 Stukas, and eighty reconnaissance planes. It was Hermann

Goering's belief, based upon the great successes enjoyed by the Luftwaffe in Poland, France, and Holland, that his short-ranged, lightly armed Heinkel and Junkers bombers could smash Britain aided only by fighter escorts. Neither he nor Hitler saw the need for long-range, four-engined bombers, and the mighty Luftwaffe thus sought to wage strategic warfare with what were essentially tactical, ground-support aircraft.

The RAF nonetheless faced formidable odds. To oppose the German armada Britain could field 400 Hawker Hurricanes and only 200 Supermarine Spitfires. The Hurricane entered active service with the RAF early in 1937, the first low-wing fighter to become operational in England. This humpbacked, fabric-covered fighter was tough and heavily armed; eight .303 Browning machine guns were packed in the wings, and the Rolls-Royce Merlin XX liquid-cooled engine drove the Hurricane to a maximum speed of 340 mph. But the "Hurry" was no match for the faster Me–109E, which could outclimb and outdive the British fighter; the Hurricane's only advantage over the Messerschmitt was its ability to turn tighter in a dogfight, and this was a purely defensive advantage. It was decided by RAF Fighter Command to employ the Hurricane, wherever possible, against the incoming German bombers, leaving duels with the Me–109s to the newer and more deadly Spitfires.

The "Spit," as pilots called it, was the most beautiful fighter ever designed. Based on the 1931 Schneider Cup winner, the Spitfire evolved from a racing seaplane that had set a speed record for floatplanes of 407.5 mph eight years before the start of World War II. The Spitfire was a study in ellipses; one curve flowed gracefully into another from the long nose to the tail, and outward to the broad, 36-foot, 10-inch wings. The powerplant, a 1,175-hp Merlin, gave the Spitfire a top speed of just over 370 mph and a ceiling of 42,000 feet. So economical of line, the elegantly tapered fuselage left little room for the pilot, encumbered as he was with uniform, heavy flying boots, seat-type parachute, and the rubber "Mae West" inflatable life jacket worn in case the pilot was forced to bail out or ditch into the Channel. Hefty pilots found that their shoulders rubbed against the sides of the cockpit, and tall pilots had to crank the seat to the full "Down" position to keep their helmeted heads from pressing against the top of the canopy. Nevertheless, Spitfire pilots would trade their agile, thoroughbred fighter for no other. Some Spitfires were fitted with 20-mm cannons, but early models were unreliable, and

Battle of Britain pilots greatly preferred the eight-gunned Spitfire IIs; the Browning machine guns were dependable and when harmonized to produce a concentration of fire at killing range no German plane could withstand the devastating firepower.

By July, British aircraft factories were turning out nearly 500 fighters per month, enough to replenish losses expected in the coming battle, but men more than machines win battles and the RAF was acutely short of trained pilots. More than 300 experienced fighter pilots had been lost during the brief but furious battle for France, and this was a loss that would be hard to make up. Pilots were pulled from Coastal Command and from Bomber Command to fill the gaps, but the fate of Britain would largely rest upon the shoulders of the few surviving old hands in their mid-twenties and upon those fresh from training schools, many of them still in their teens.

These pilots, however, had one great technical advantage over the Germans that the enemy did not suspect they had—radar. Strung along England's

Willy Messerschmitt's contribution to the Luftwaffe was the fast, agile Me–109, that in various modifications, saw service during World War II from the first day to the last.

eastern coast were twenty of these radar stations, conspicuous by their tall towers, capable of detecting the approach of German formations as far as 100 miles away. Observers bent over their cathode-ray tubes were able to determine the course, speed, and approximate number of bombers headed for England. This information was fed to RAF controllers, who thus were able to deploy the squadrons of Fighter Command so that they wasted neither time nor fuel in making intercepts.

But above all, the youthful British fighter pilots' greatest advantage was the fact that they were fighting above their homeland. Every bomber they shot down meant so many fewer bombs that would come crashing down into the streets of English towns. Already Hitler was assembling invasion barges on the coast of France, and if the Luftwaffe gained control of English skies there would be little to keep hundreds of thousands of storm troopers from storming ashore to crush the population, just as they had in Poland, Holland, Belgium, Denmark, Norway, and France. Never in history had so few men such great reason for giving so much.

The first phase of the Battle of Britain opened on the morning of July 10 with an attack by seventy German planes upon a small British convoy steaming slowly up the English Channel. The RAF, knowing that the main event would be fought out over England itself, held back its main fighter force. Six Hurricanes on routine patrol in the vicinity of the convoy waded into the swirling mass of German planes with guns blazing. Minutes later, twenty Spitfires and Hurricanes joined the combat, cutting the odds, but leaving them still two-to-one. Headlong attacks by the British fighters finally drove the Germans back across the Channel, but only after three Hurricanes had been shot down and one of the ships bombed to the bottom of the sea. The Germans lost four Me–109s, but the surviving pilots were jubilant; the RAF seemed to be powerless to send up more than a few fighters at a time, and these were mostly Hurricanes, no match for Messerschmitts.

Combats above the Channel raged throughout the month of July. The Germans hammered at the convoys hugging the coast of England, but sinking ships was only incidental to the Luftwaffe's primary goal: to draw the bulk of Fighter Command into battle and destroy it. But the RAF knew that the main battle lay ahead, and only minimum numbers of fighters were committed over the Channel to deal with the Stukas and the Ju–88s that were giving British ships such a pasting. Even so, by the end of July more than 100 German planes had been shot down, but RAF losses were nearly half that many, and so many ships had been sunk or damaged that the Royal Navy hesitated to send even destroyers into a Channel that had become a watery graveyard for pilots and sailors alike.

On August 1, *Reichsmarschall* Hermann Goering (known as "Fatso" to pilots on both sides) declared that the battle for the Channel was over. He ordered his group and squadrons commanders to prepare for the knockout blow against England. Goering assured Hitler that Fighter Command would have no choice but to commit everything to the defense of the homeland. Then, Goering said, it would all be over with in four days.

At Fighter Command bases such as Debden, Biggin Hill, Manston, Tangmere, Kenly, and Duxford, Spitfire and Hurricane pilots waited in readiness. Some sat in chairs on the edge of the airfields, their planes waiting only yards away. Others sat in ready rooms, playing cards or writing letters. All were impatient, and a few were angry because they had been kept in reserve while others had been in combat with the Germans. They wondered when their turn would come.

On the morning of August 15, the Germans struck. Nearly a thousand Luftwaffe bombers and fighters converged on Britain from bases as far north as Norway and as far south as the Brittany peninsula. There were so many German formations on the radar tubes that the controllers were hard-pressed to know where to direct the main fighter strengths. Aerial battles were

The mainstay of German aerial offensive against the British Isles was the Heinkel 111, seen here in mass formation headed for London on a daylight raid. Note gun turrets top and bottom, mounting only single machine guns. Defensive armament was He–111's weakest point.

Finest German medium bomber of World War II was the Junkers 88, a fast, tough plane that dealt heavy blows to British shipping in the Channel during the opening phase of the Battle of Britain.

fought in an arc more than 500 miles wide. The earphones in fighter pilots' helmets crackled with information about German dispositions. "Twenty-plus bandits approaching Harwich at angels eighteen. Steer nine-zero." Minutes later, the figure would be upped to thirty, then fifty bandits. Hurricanes and Spitfires clawed for altitude, hoping to get to the packed bomber formations before escorting Me–109s could drop out of the sun to block them off.

As the pattern of the massive raid developed, it became clear to the ground controllers and to Fighter Command that the worst fears of the RAF were being realized; the Germans had started the blitz on fighter stations and radar posts. Kenly Airdrome was subjected to a devastating low-level attack by Ju–88s, followed by a more leisurely bombing by He–111s flying at 12,000 feet. The earth shook as the big bombs tore into the runways, blasted hangars, set fire to fuel reserves, and demolished barracks. Reserve Spitfires and those in maintenance hangars were wrecked by direct hits or were badly damaged by low-level strafing.

The Germans concentrated their attacks on the forward airfields, most of them within five miles of the coast. Lympne, Manston, and Hawkinge were hit by a mixed force of more than a hundred Stukas and Me–109s. After the Stukas had unloaded their bombs, they stayed around with the Messerschmitts to strafe everything in sight from treetop level. Precious fighters were destroyed on the ground, and scores of men and women were killed and

The Luftwaffe had high hopes for the twin-engined Me–110 as an escort fighter, but its design proved inadequate for daylight missions due to lack of speed, maneuverability and poor armament. They were easy prey for Spits and Hurricanes.

wounded. The whine of engines, the thudding of bombs, and the crackle of machine guns lasted until late in the afternoon, when the Luftwaffe went home. Although seventy-four German aircraft had been shot down, Fighter Command lost thirty-four Spitfires and Hurricanes in the day's bitter fighting.

The assault resumed at noon the next day under hot, clear skies. Aloft over southern England on standing patrol was a section of three Hurricanes of 249 Squadron, led by Flight Lieutenant J. B. Nicholson, a fiery Yorkshireman who so far had been denied a victory over the Germans. Near Southhampton, Nicholson's heart raced as he saw a gang of Ju–88s streaking inland. Nicholson dived for the bombers, but Spitfires beat him to the attack, coming apparently from nowhere. As Nicholson started climbing back for altitude he failed to see a twin-engined Me–110—probably part of the Ju–88 escort—slide in behind him and fasten its sights on his tail. The next thing Nicholson felt was a hail of bullets thudding into the wings and fuselage of his Hurricane, then blinding pain and slugs struck him in the leg and grazed his head. Nicholson reacted by throwing the Hurricane into a steep bank.

Through a haze of blood seeping from underneath his helmet, the British fighter pilot watched as the Me-110 shot past. Now flames leaped back from the Hurricane's engine and quickly began eating away at the fabric-covered fuselage. Badly wounded and his plane on fire, Nicholson should have released his belt, shoved back the canopy and flipped on his back to fall free of the flaming fighter. Flames had eaten through the firewall and Nicholson's hands and arms were seared, but he bore on after the German plane, one burned hand shoving the throttle forward, the other pressing against the stick. He glued the nose of his burning fighter on the outline of the Me-110, and when the enemy plane filled his sights Nicholson pressed the firing button. His eight Brownings chugged, and Nicholson saw the other plane stagger, then dive down into the sea.

Nicholson painfully managed to undo his seat belt and get the canopy back. Unbearable heat beat against his face until he struggled free of the cockpit and began tumbling through space. He clawed at the D-ring with his charred hands, and finally managed to pull the ripcord that allowed the white silk parachute to deploy. Nicholson was a bundle of pain as he drifted slowly to earth, but he managed to keep consciousness. As he prepared for the landing shock he noticed that a great many men were streaming onto the field where he would hit. Thank God, Nicholson thought to himself, it would not be long before he was being rushed to hospital by friendly hands. Nicholson's relief turned to fear, then outrage, as he watched the men on the ground raise shotguns and rifles to the sky. They were aiming at him!

Many fighter pilots had been afraid of what was about to happen to Nicholson. England, expecting invasion every minute, had organized elements of the Home Guard composed of those too old or too young to join the armed forces. Fowling pieces, stag rifles, and even pitchforks formed the arsenals of these volunteer guardsmen, all of whom were ready and willing to blast German paratroopers from the skies.

As Nicholson came within range he began shouting to the ground, but was greeted by a ragged barrage. Nicholson could hear the rifle slugs cracking as they went past, then he felt a sting as a few pellets from a shotgun blast struck his leg. Fortunately, the Home Guardsmen stopped firing when Nicholson hit the ground. Shocked at what they had almost done, the old gentlemen who had tried to kill Nicholson rushed him to the nearest hospital, where he was treated for his burns and given a transfusion. Nicholson, who forgave the guards, survived to receive the Victoria Cross, Britain's highest award for valor, the only one given during the Battle of Britain.

Australian Wing Commander G. G. C. Olive had survived a heavy German attack upon the airdrome where his Spitfires were stationed, and was at altitude seeking a gaggle of German bombers when his oxygen system literally exploded, making a shambles out of the cockpit. Olive bailed out and reached the ground safely, only to be charged by a group of farm girls wielding pitchforks, rakes, and hoes. Despite Olive's Aussie accent he managed to convince the girls he was actually on their side. An ambulance was summoned to take him to a nearby hospital for routine examination, but hardly was the ambulance on the road when the eager driver overshot a turn and the vehicle skidded into a ditch, coming to rest upside down. Olive crawled out nursing cuts and bruises, then stood waiting for new transportation. A few minutes later a fire engine appeared, headed for the site of Olive's burning Spitfire. Olive got aboard, thinking that at last he would make it to the hospital. Moments later, however, the fire engine went out of control and plunged off the road. Olive groggily left the wreck holding an injured arm and started walking. Flying, he decided, was far safer than riding about with the saviors of the fire and ambulance brigades.

As Spitfires and Hurricanes did their work, the English countryside became littered with hulks of German bombers knocked out of the sky. This He–111 failed to make it back to Germany after mission over London.

The Luftwaffe's massed formations broke through the thin defense screens thrown up by the British fighters, who had to be everywhere at once; the Germans were always able to get a certain number of bombers over the target, but they were paying a price. Especially vulnerable were the once-fearsome Stukas. Once they went into their steep dives it was impossible for the cleaner, swifter Me–109s to fly slowly enough to provide close-in escort. The Stukas became easy prey for Spitfires and Hurricanes and so many were shot down during the furious air battles of mid-August that Goering withdrew them from the fighting altogether.

Bad weather temporarily halted the incessant German attacks on August 18, giving the RAF a desperately needed breather. Fighter Command totaled its losses since the battle began: 213 Spitfires and Hurricanes had been destroyed in the air and on the ground. Although the factories, working round-the-clock shifts, struggled to turn out fighters faster than they were lost, they were slipping behind. More critical was the loss of pilots. Fewer than seventy new fighter pilots were being fed into the grinder each week. Although the Germans were being hurt worse than the RAF, they could well afford the losses so long as Fighter Command appeared to dwindle. It was an air war of attrition, and the Germans were winning.

When the weather improved, the Luftwaffe came against England in increasing fury. Fighter escorts were beefed up until there were three Me–109s for every German bomber. Fighter bases in England were hit again and again, and the surviving RAF pilots flew to the point of exhaustion, some of them making as many as five intercept missions in one day. It required tough, dedicated men to stand up to the grueling demands imposed by the seemingly endless German attacks, and a New Zealand Squadron Leader named Al C. Deere typified the sheer courage and endurance possessed by the men of Fighter Command during those dark days of summer. How Al Deere survived is a miracle.

During a chase after a Do–17 near the French coast both the bomber and Deere's Spitfire were riddled with bullets. The bomber crash-landed, and so did Deere. He was knocked out by the impact, and came to in time to crawl away only seconds before the Spit exploded. Two days later Deere was dueling with an Me–109 over the Channel. The German was as brave as Deere, and when the two fighters were on a collision course, coming at each other head-on with a combined speed of more than 600 mph, neither would give way. The Messerschmitt's belly scraped across the top of Deere's Spitfire, snapping the propeller and jamming the canopy on top of Deere's head. Deere, blinded by smoke and flames, turned the crippled Spitfire around and glided for England at only 100 mph. He managed to reach the coast, but crashed against a concrete anti-invasion post, ripped off a wing, skidded through two fields of corn and came to rest blazing. Deere somehow managed to get out and drag himself to safety.

Two days later, Deere was jumped by a swarm of Me–109s who shot his plane to pieces. Deere's watch was shot off his wrist and a second slug grazed his head. Deere flew back as far as Ashford, twenty miles inland, and was at 800 feet when the Spitfire began to fall apart. Deere bailed out, his chute opening only a few feet from the ground. He was flying again the next day, and within less than two weeks had been shot down three more times, once in flames, and once coming down in his parachute in a plum tree.

While getting ready to take off from his airdrome, Deere watched as the Germans came in at low level to string their bombs the length of the runway. A bomb exploded just in front of Deere's Spitfire, flinging the plane upside down and into a skid for 150 feet along the ground. Deere, with his head in the grass and the cockpit filling with fuel from the ruptured gas line, helplessly waited for the inevitable fire and explosion, but helping hands dragged him away before he could be incinerated. Deere was ordered to bed to rest, but when the sirens began to wail again, he jumped out of bed, got into his Spitfire and took off to shoot down a Dornier.

That afternoon Deere was aloft with a new pilot, trying to teach him the tricks of the trade needed to survive. The pupil miscalculated a practice attack on Deere's plane and rammed his instructor's Spitfire just forward of the tail. Deere's fighter was cut in half, and he spun wildly out of control, unable to get clear until the Spitfire was only a few thousand feet above the earth. When Deere finally fought clear of the cockpit he discovered that his parachute harness was partially torn off and that the D-ring was dangling out of reach. Deere closed his eyes, waiting for the final impact with the ground. Then he was suddenly jerked upright. Amazed, he looked up and saw the canopy billowing over his head; the chute had opened by itself.

Despite Al Deere's constant brushes with death, he managed to fight on,

Familiar to RAF pilots in the air and to civilians on the ground was the Dornier 217E, known as the "Flying Pencil." This Do–217 was shot down, then broke its back in crash landing.

and from May through August 1940, he was credited with shooting down 17 German fighters and bombers. Men like these saved England.

The renewed German offensive on British fighter airfields slowly ate away at the reserves of planes and pilots, and Fighter Command knew that unless some miracle happened the day was not far off when England would have so few fighters left that the Luftwaffe would be virtually unopposed. That miracle occurred when a German bomber squadron on a night mission became confused and instead of unloading their bombs on oil storage tanks along the Thames river dropped them on the city of London, destroying homes and killing civilians. Within twenty-four hours Berlin was bombed for the first time in the war by a force of twin-engined RAF bombers. Hitler then made one of his greatest mistakes: he ordered Goering to call off the successful attacks upon British fighter stations and to throw the entire might of the Luftwaffe instead upon London. Any rules heretofore observed about indiscriminate bombing of large cities were scrapped. Hitler planned to terrorize the English into submission.

The raids began on September 7 and kept coming by day and by night until the greatest battle of all was fought over the greatest city in the world on September 15. The Luftwaffe sent more than a thousand bombers and 700 fighters against London from noon until dusk. Homes, hospitals, office buildings, schools, docks, gasworks, telephone exchanges, and other targets were ripped apart by the bombers that got through, but Fighter Command destroyed sixty German planes, while losing only twenty-six of their own.

Now that the Germans were penetrating farther inland than before, their handicaps rose. An Me–109 was very short-ranged, being able to stay over London less than thirty minutes after the climb-out from bases in France. Pilots who overstayed their time ran the risk of not getting back home; in fact, on one hard-fought mission over London Messerschmitt pilots took too great a gamble and nine of them were forced to ditch in the Channel when their tanks ran dry. Spitfire and Hurricane pilots, on the other hand, could fight until fuel and ammunition were nearly gone, then land to refuel and rearm and be back in action almost immediately. When German pilots and crewmen bailed out of crippled planes they were captured, their combat days at an end; but RAF fighter pilots bailed out over friendly territory and often were fighting again the same day.

Close view of damage inflicted by RAF fighter upon Me–109 shot down over England and sent on tour to gather contributions for the RAF orphan's fund. Note 20-mm cannon and .303 caliber holes. Signatures scratched on German paint are those of English civilians.

Although the Londoners suffered terribly under the bombs, Fighter Command was able to replenish its losses, and since the fields were now free of attack, every squadron was airborne against the Luftwaffe. By September 17, Hitler knew that he had lost the battle. He called off the proposed invasion of the British Isles, and although daylight raids continued until the end of September these, too, had to be canceled. Afterwards the German crews only came at night to sow destruction on English villages and cities.

By October 31, the Battle of Britain was at an end. It had cost the lives of 450 RAF pilots and 915 planes. Thousands of civilians were dead. The Germans lost 1,733 aircraft during the battle, and only afterwards did they realize that they had lost much more. By failing to bring Fighter Command to its knees, the Germans lost their opportunity to win a decisive victory in a war that would continue for nearly five more years.

Eagle Squadron pilots cut their teeth in combat while flying Spitfires. American volunteer pilots couldn't wait for their own country to commit itself in the war against Nazi Germany, and found ways to reach Canada, then England, then the cockpits of RAF fighters.

4/EAGLES HAVE WINGS

EVEN AS THE BATTLE OF BRITAIN was deciding the outcome of the war, most of America remained asleep and unaware of the very real danger of Nazi Germany taking over half of the world. Those who were not dozing had every sympathy for the ordinary man then being lashed by fire and steel throughout England, but because Congress had declared the United States officially "neutral," there seemed little that the most sympathetic citizen could do to help his British cousins far across the Atlantic.

However, a select few young American men have always found a way to pitch in and help the underdog and to find an outlet for the spirit of adventure that runs deep in a fortunate handful. In 1836 Kentuckians and Tennesseans journeyed all the way to Texas to, as Davy Crockett put it, "fight for their rights." In 1914, when America was even more determinedly neutral than in 1939, hundreds of young Americans volunteered for the French Foreign Legion, earning a penny a day. Some of these found their way into the select ranks of the Lafayette Escadrille as America's first fighter pilots, and it was from the combat-hardened Americans who flew with the French that the United States was later able to form the nucleus of its first all-U.S. squadrons. As it was in 1916, so it would be again in 1940.

Newsreels, radio broadcasts, and daily newspaper accounts of the stirring aerial combats being waged over England sent Americans for the Canadian border, where they hoped to enlist in the RAF. The Canadians were glad to have them, but at first many were turned back by U.S. authorities who cautioned the eager volunteers against violating the Neutrality Act. Two veteran World War I pilots, among many, joined in to help those trying to get into the fighting. Elliott White Springs, the colorful cotton baron from South Carolina and a 1918 Sopwith Camel pilot with twelve Germans to his

43

credit, often took his private railroad car to the big turntable underneath the Waldorf-Astoria Hotel in New York City and there met with one of his cronies, Clayton Knight, a one-time DH–9 pilot. Both Springs and Knight had trained and fought with the British Royal Flying Corps, and they understood the yearnings of the aspiring warriors, helping many to reach Canada. When the Neutrality Act was finally dropped, the United States allowed RAF recruiters to put up booths outside Army Air Force pilot-training centers, where the British could catch rejected cadets on the bounce. One way or another more than two hundred Americans reached the other side of the friendly border to earn their wings, enabling them to fly in combat with the 71st, 121st, or 133rd Eagle Squadron.

The Eagles came from a variety of backgrounds. One had been a Lockheed test pilot, another a film studio guide in Hollywood, one a former U.S. Navy pilot, some came straight out of high schools or colleges, and a few had been commercial or private pilots. About the only thing the Eagles had in common was a love for the sky and, as one of them put it, a desire "to do a little job of work for England."

Don Salvatore Gentile, of Piqua, Ohio, was one of these men. Gentile's father had emigrated to the United States from Italy when he was fourteen and worked his way up from a water boy in a gas company to foreman, earning sixty dollars a week. He was generous with his family, and often gave young Don a five-dollar bill to take a girl out on a date. But Don's only passion was flying; and he never spent more than a dollar out of his allowance; the rest he put into the bank to save for flying lessons and, sooner or later, an airplane of his own. When Gentile was eighteen he finally became the proud owner of an Aerosport biplane. He was up flying every Saturday when the weather was clear, buzzing his girl friends' houses and generally beating up the town. Police cars vainly chased the twisting, turning biplane, but were never able to get Gentile's registration number in order to take his license away. He had a passion for speed, often driving his dad's Zephyr sedan over lonely roads at 100 mph. "Catch me if you can," was his byword. Gentile explained that every man needs competition in order to feel alive, and getting the most out of a machine was his own kind of competition.

In September 1940, when the Battle of Britain was at its peak, Don Gentile enlisted in the RAF and made his way to Canada where he won his wings. Early in 1942 he was sent to England, where his skill at the controls of a Spitfire convinced the authorities that this lean, dark, hawk-nosed young

American would make an ideal instructor. Gentile wanted to fight, not instruct. He climbed into his Spitfire and buzzed a dog track where a race was in progress. Greyhounds and bettors scattered in all directions, and when Gentile returned to his airdrome he was put on the carpet and thoroughly chastised. But he won his point; no longer did the authorities believe that twenty-one-year-old Gentile had the temperament to make an instructor. He was assigned to the 133rd Eagle Squadron, where he slowly learned what war was all about.

Gentile flew his first combat mission on June 22, 1942. The 133rd was ordered on a sweep over the French coastal town of Boulogne. The Spitfires flashed across the flat gray slate of the Channel, and as they neared the enemy coast Gentile's cockiness drained away. He remembered asking himself, *What am I doing up here? I'm only a kid!* His mind leapt back to the comfortable frame house in Ohio, and he thought of his wonderful Italian mama. Gentile's reverie was shattered by a cry in his earphones. "Break! Break! They're bouncing us! Break, you damn fool!" Gentile horsed the stick and rudder around, almost graying-out from the G-load, trying desperately to stay glued to his element leader's wing. The next few minutes were a confusion of screaming engines, the distant popping of machine guns, of seeing the horizon and the sky and the brown earth blend in a whirling mass.

Crippled in raid across the Channel, this Spitfire made it back to crash-land on an English field. Spit came to a stop in four parts, but pilot lived to tell the tale.

Throughout the combat Gentile saw nothing except the elliptical wing of his element leader's Spitfire. When they landed back in England, Gentile was pale with excitement and tension. Only then did he learn that the 133rd had lost some pilots and that the Germans had, too.

Gentile was hesitant and unsure of himself throughout his next month of combat. He had only two thoughts: to stick with his element leader, and to stay alive. Then, on July 31, Don Gentile became a fighter pilot. The squadron was bounced by a dozen of the new German fighters, Focke-Wulf 190s, shortly after the Eagles crossed the French coast. Gentile knew immediately that they were in trouble; the FW–190s had their engine cowlings painted bright yellow, identifying them as the crack group of fighter pilots based at Abbeville. The FW–190 could reach nearly 400 mph, was heavily armed with two machine guns and four 20-mm cannon and could climb like a bat. It was superior in every way to the Spitfire V that Gentile was flying, except in one important detail: the Spit could outturn a 190, and it was this ability that saved Gentile's life.

The "Abbeville Kids," as these particular Germans were called, bounced the Eagles at 30,000 feet. Half of the 190s hit the Spits head-on, the other half from the rear. Gentile watched his element leader go down almost immediately, then saw that one of the Huns had fastened his yellow nose on his own tail. Gentile knew that the more experienced German could best him in a duel, but instead of panicking, Gentile coolly decided to pit his own athletic body against that of the German. He shoved the stick forward, adding aileron, and started a steep spiral dive six miles above the earth. Gentile intentionally tightened his turns to such a point that punishing G-loads caused

Two cannons and a pair of machine guns gave the FW–190 a heavy punch, as American fighter and bomber crews learned—the hard way.

During bloody raid on Dieppe in 1942, Eagle Squadron pilots dueled with German planes such as this Dornier 217, seen here as it looked to Canadian and English troops fighting for their lives on the French beach.

him to black out repeatedly. Just before losing consciousness each time, Gentile would ease off the stick, then tighten up again. Gentile won the brutal contest, for when he pulled out just above the deck he saw that he was alone. "After cheating that Hun out of his piece of cake," Gentile recalled, "I began to get confidence that even if I couldn't make the pace in the game I at least had a chance to go along with it."

Gentile did much more than that. On August 19, 1942, British Commandos and Canadian regulars stormed the beaches at the resort town of Dieppe. The Eagle Squadrons were among those providing fighter protection for the struggling raiders below. The infantrymen were being shot to pieces by the Germans, and within a few hours it was all over, a massacre. But in the air it was a different story; the Luftwaffe was kept at bay by the RAF, preventing even worse casualties.

Gentile spotted a Ju–88 headed down to bomb and strafe the beach. He slipped his Spitfire underneath the German's blind spot, then pulled up and raked the bomber with his eight guns. The German pilot jettisoned his bombs harmlessly in the water and desperately tried to escape Gentile's fighter. Gentile closed in, threw a "barnful" of bullets at the enemy plane, then watched it lurch in the air and crash in flames on the beach. Gentile regained altitude, then saw a pair of yellow-nosed FW–190s below. He got the sun at his back, and dived. One of the Focke-Wulfs went down immediately, but the other managed to escape by pouring on maximum throttle, leaving Gentile's slower Spitfire behind, still firing.

Gentile's earlier caution was now blended with supreme confidence, and

Close view of He–111 reveals excellent visibility "greenhouse" provided German bombadier. This shot-down Heinkel was flown from one RAF base to another to allow British fighter pilots to study the nature of the enemy machine at first hand. White area beneath fuselage indicates wartime censorship of a British fighter with modifications meant to be kept secret from the enemy.

the combination enabled the "kid" from Ohio to become one of the world's top fighter pilots.

At about the same time that Gentile was bagging his first two Germans, another Eagle Squadron pilot was floating down to the Channel in a parachute, firing a pistol wildly into the sea. This Eagle, who had his wings clipped, was Chesley Gordon Peterson, a Squadron Leader, ace and holder of the British Distinguished Flying Cross at the age of only twenty-two. Peterson was thin and lanky, long-legged and hatchet-faced. He had a shock of sandy, wavy hair and a gentle smile and he spoke in soft tones. He was seldom seen without a battered briar pipe clenched between his teeth; the pipe, he felt, made him seem older, a father figure to the "boys" he commanded.

Peterson was one of the "washouts" who joined the RAF when his own country informed him that he "lacked flying ability." When the U.S. Army Air Corps lost, the RAF gained. Peterson was one of the original members of the first Eagle Squadron, the 71st, that went into action against the Germans in May 1941. Peterson quickly worked himself up to Squadron Commander, shooting down five Germans in the process, but the Eagles took some hard knocks while learning their trade. Returning from a sweep over France, Pilot Officer J. J. Lynch was forced so low to the deck that his Spitfire clipped a wooden telephone post, shearing three feet from the wing, but Lynch made it back home. Others were not so lucky. By the end of the 71st Squadron's first year in combat, twelve of its pilots had been shot down.

Over Dieppe on that hot August morning, Peterson bored in on the tail of a Ju–88. The German gunner swung his machine gun at Peterson's Spitfire at the same time that the American pressed Button A. Peterson felt the strikes on his fighter as he watched his own tracers eating into the Junker's cockpit. The Spitfire's Merlin engine blew up and started blazing at the same time the Ju–88 rolled over on its back and headed for a grave in the Channel. Peterson slid the canopy back, undid his seat belt, rolled the burning fighter on its back, and fell free. When the Spitfire spiraled away a safe distance, Peterson hauled on the D-ring and felt the comforting jerk as the white silk billowed out. As Peterson drifted toward the water he began checking his straps and prepared to inflate his Mae West. Then Peterson's hand found the .38 Webley-Vickers service revolver all pilots wore. It was new, unfired, tempting. Figuring that the pistol would shortly be ruined by a dunking in salt water, Peterson decided to let the pistol "see action" at Dieppe. He drew it from the leather shoulder holster and pointed it at the Channel and began firing, enjoying every shot until the chamber was empty. Then he threw the pistol away and splashed into the sea. Twenty minutes later he was picked up by a rescue boat, given a blanket and a tot of rum, and soon was back in England.

The three Eagle Squadrons stayed in combat with the Royal Air Force until September 29, 1942. America had been at war with Germany almost a year, but it wasn't until that date that the U.S. Army Air Force was ready to receive its own citizens into the Eighth Fighter Command. The Eagles were transferred en masse to the 4th Fighter Group, where many of them went on to achieve high scores and great honors.

Officially, the pilots of the 71st, 121st, and 133rd Eagle Squadrons were credited with 73½ kills, but nearly a hundred of them were shot down and killed themselves, or sweated out dreary months and years of German prison camps. As RAF pilot officers, they were paid less than eighty dollars per month, and nobody could ever say that they had not earned it.

49

Westland Lysander was versatile RAF reconaissance craft in desert warfare. High-sitting pilot had excellent visibility downwards, could even drop bombs from special racks installed just above wheel covers.

5/WAR IN THE DESERT

ADOLF HITLER's partner in world crime was strutting Benito Mussolini, who hoped to share in the German spoils of war—but without taking great risks. On June 10, 1940, with France all but crushed by the German blitzkrieg, Mussolini declared war on France and Great Britain. Commented President Franklin D. Roosevelt: "The hand that held the dagger has struck it into the back of its neighbor." Mussolini dreamed, above all, of conquering all of North Africa; he wanted the vital Suez Canal controlled by Fascist Italy. The canal was Britain's lifeline, her only sea route to survival for the dark days that lay ahead. Britain was determined that Egypt and the Suez would be denied to this new enemy. Winston Churchill ordered the Empire's only armored division to Africa, but because the Battle of Britain was beginning, the Royal Air Force could not immediately reinforce the understrength air groups already in North Africa. The Italians could throw at the British 310 bombers and 260 fighters, while the Desert Air Force could muster only 40 Gladiator biplanes, 70 Blenheim bombers, 24 Westland Lysander reconnaissance craft, and ten of the clumsy Sunderland flying boats. Recalled Air Chief Marshal Sir Arthur William Tedder, "Faced with great numerical inferiority on every front, the RAF took the only possible course—the offensive." On the day Italy declared war, the RAF attacked Italian airdromes in Libya, bombing and strafing Savoia-Marchetti 79 bombers, Fiat CR–42 biplane fighters, and the newer and more dangerous Macchi-Castoldi 200 fighters that were lined up in inviting rows on the unsuspecting airfields. From that day forward, despite the reinforcement of Italian air power, the RAF never lost the initiative in the air.

On September 13, 1940, the Italian army moved eastward across the dunes out of Libya to invade Egypt. They counted heavily upon the *Regia Aeronautica* to help pave the way, but the RAF had been reinforced with thirteen squadrons, including forty Hurricanes, and the Italians were beaten back both on the ground and in the air.

51

On December 9, the British Eighth Army began a counteroffensive, and within sixty-two days the Italians were crushed. More than 1,000 destroyed Italian planes—most of them shot up on the ground—were counted by the advancing British on their way to the sea. How air power, and especially the fighters, made the British infantry and armored advance possible was summed up by Air Marshal Tedder shortly after the battle. "Before each Army assault the bombers attacked in turn Sidi Barrani, Bardia, Tobruk, Derna, and Bengazi; but these bombing raids would scarcely have been possible had not our fighters pinned down the Italian fighter force and kept it on the defensive. The strafing of the aerodromes and the roads did that, and on their homeward journeys, our fighters often encountered the unescorted Italian bombers which were trying to give support to their troops. We shot down seventy-four enemy aircraft during the first week of the advance alone."

Before the Italians could be totally driven from the desert, the Germans came to their rescue. In March 1941, the first of the famed *Afrika Korps* divisions and elements of the Luftwaffe were landed in North Africa. The Germans were determined to accomplish what the Italians had bungled. The Luftwaffe put into battle fast Ju–88s, Me–109Es and the standby of German infantry support, Ju–87D Stukas. In theory, the Stuka was an ideal weapon for the war in the desert, where targets were usually the "pinpoint" variety—tank squadrons, fixed emplacements, motor-transport parks, fuel and ammunition dumps. How the Stuka fared in this new battlefield disappointed even its staunchest supporters; British fighters shot more Stukas out of the sky than were able to reach and bomb assigned targets successfully.

When the Germans failed to defeat Fighter Command during the Battle of Britain, the pressure eased and soon the factories were able to provide the Desert Air Force with sufficient numbers of improved Spitfires and Hurricanes to deal with the Me–109s, against whom the old Gloster Gladiators were no match. The RAF was further beefed up by fighters manufactured and supplied by the United States. The British received large numbers of Curtiss P–40E Kittyhawks, greatly improved versions of the original P–40 that entered service with the U.S. Army Air Forces early in 1940. The Kittyhawk was powered by a 12–cylinder Allison in-line liquid-cooled engine and could reach a top speed of 335 mph at low altitude, where it was designed to operate. The Kittyhawk had a much slower rate of climb than the

Billowing clouds of sand kicked up by propwash from RAF Kittyhawk in Western Desert so obscured pilots' vision that ground crewmen often rode wingtip to guide pilot to takeoff point.

Me–109E, it was not nearly as maneuverable, but it packed a solid punch: six .50-caliber guns were in the wings, and "Kittybombers," as they were called, could be loaded with a pair of 100–pound bombs under the wings and a 500–pound bomb slung underneath the fuselage. Thus they were ideal tank-busters, as Field Marshal Erwin Rommel was to discover during the seesaw battles that raged back and forth across the desert.

Rommel was a tank general who did not fully appreciate the value of air power as a supporting arm of his panzers, and the Luftwaffe was never fully put to its most effective use during the entire North African campaign. Of course, the poor British foot soldiers who were strafed and dive-bombed by German aircraft snarling overhead would say that even a little German air-power applied in the right place was too much; but the fact remains that had Rommel used the Luftwaffe to its fullest the desert war would have been much tougher for his opponents.

As it was, the Luftwaffe caused many casualties among the English, Australian, South African, and Polish fliers. The most deadly German pilot in the Western Desert was a one-man wave of destruction who, during his brief but spectacular career, destroyed the equivalent of seventeen squadrons of British fighters. His name was Hans-Joachim Marseilles, and when he reported for duty in North Africa he was twenty-one years old and probably the least popular member of his unit *Jagdgeschwader* 27.

Marseilles, a lean, large-eyed youth with black hair combed straight back in the German fashion, was a renegade. He was as tense as a violin string, resentful of authority, and exploded in anger when denied his way. Fond of pretty girls and hot jazz music, Marseilles gave the first impression of a frustrated playboy more suited to a life of beer halls and sports cars than as a team member of a German fighter squadron. Instead of the customary drab flying boots most pilots wore, Marseilles wore white tennis shoes into combat. Of course this gave him more sensitivity of feel on the rudder pedals and kept his feet cooler, but some of his fellow pilots thought that he was merely eccentric. After a few weeks of combat they changed their minds.

Once Marseilles was airborne in his Me–109E all trace of nervousness vanished; his flying was silk-smooth, his hot blood turned cold, and his shooting was incredible. Constant practice, "dry runs" in tracking anything that moved with his sights, made Marseilles one of the deadliest marksmen in the Luftwaffe. On June 6, 1942, Marseilles coolly dispatched six P–40s in less than twelve minutes. Four days later he shot down four Spitfires over Bir

Hakeim to run his score to eighty-one, and within the next week, twenty-one more British planes were downed to raise his kills to 101. Against his will, Marseilles was sent back to Germany on enforced leave, but he was back in the desert at the end of August, ready to go back to work.

Marseilles flew through almost every daylight hour on September 1, making three sorties that day and shooting down no fewer than seventeen British airplanes. During the last week of the month, he raised his score to 158, all air-to-air kills, then on September 1 luck ran out for the "Star of Africa." Returning from a routine escort mission, Marseilles' engine burst into flames and when he went over the side his parachute failed and he streaked to his death on the desert floor.

By the late fall of 1942, the United States was ready to begin offensive operations against the Germans. The move westward against the Japanese in the Pacific Ocean got under way with the landing of the 1st Marine Division at Guadalcanal in August, and now, three months later, the United States was ready to move against the other half of the Axis powers. On November 8, American and British infantry went ashore at three separate points in Morocco and in Algeria. The German Afrika Korps was thus a tough nut caught between a pair of crackers, and once the enemy was defeated in Africa, not only would the Suez Canal be safe, but the Allies would be in a position to invade Hitler's Europe from the south, through what Winston Churchill called "the soft underbelly."

American air power in North Africa was under the command of the U.S. 12th Air Force, composed largely of P–40 fighters and twin-engined North American B–25 Mitchell medium bombers. Later in the fighting, the 12th was reinforced with P–38s and B–24 heavy bombers, but initially the battle to cripple Rommel was waged by a relative handful of American planes. Before American factories could make their weight felt in the desert, an American staff officer made an estimate of the strengths of the air forces then in North Africa:

	German	Italian	British	American
Fighters	160	380	544	62
Light Bombers	125	25	339	46
Heavy Bombers	192	8	41	52
Total	477	413	924	160

THREE THAT CAME A CROPPER
The desert became a graveyard for Axis aircraft.

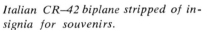

Italian CR–42 biplane stripped of insignia for souvenirs.

Ju–87 Stuka flown to a crash landing by Italians.

Gutted Me–110 being examined by Tommy of British Eighth Army.

The RAF pilots and commanders were veterans of the campaign, and they gladly provided the newer Americans with the benefit of their experience. The Yanks were willing learners, and it was not long before they made their presence felt among the Luftwaffe.

One of the most colorful characters to appear on the scene was Major Phil Cochran, who discovered that he would have to take matters into his own hands in order to come to grips with his German opponents. Cochran was a squadron commander with the 33rd Fighter Group, whose P–40 Warhawks had been launched from aircraft carriers three days after the first infantry landings. Cochran's outfit was at first flown to a remote base in Palestine— entirely too far from the fighting to suit Cochran. On a pretext, Cochran ordered his Warhawks flown right back to Africa. His superiors, instead of applauding the major's aggressive attitude, took his airplanes away from him and ordered his pilots dispersed to other squadrons. The colonels and brigadiers, thinking they had rid themselves of this brash fighter pilot, forgot all about Cochran until he started making a reputation for himself as a top organizer of men.

Cochran attached himself to a lackluster Warhawk squadron operating from an orphan airbase in Tunisia. The squadron, he discovered, lacked efficient leadership and the morale of the pilots, some of them Americans and some of them Free French, had plummeted to rock bottom. Here, Cochran, thought to himself, is a real challange. His own buoyant spirits and fighting attitude electrified the disorganized fighter pilots. He demonstrated that he could fly P–40s as well as any of them, and impressed upon them that he was not interested in personal victories by risking the squadron in man-to-man duels with the faster and more agile Me–109s, but intended to employ the P–40s to damage the enemy where it would hurt them the most, on the ground. To further boost the morale of his men, to make them feel that they were something special, Cochran bought a supply of red silk scarves and ordered his pilots to wear them. Thus Cochran's "Red Scarf Guerrillas" were born.

Cochran and his executive officer, aggressive Captain Levi Chase, jeeped across the desert and introduced themselves to the Free French forces operating in that part of Tunisia, telling them that if the French would help find enemy targets, the Red Scarf Guerrillas would take them out. "Gradually," Cochran said, "we became big operators." When the French informed

Cochran of an enemy convoy racing across the desert he got his Warhawks into the air and on top of the long lines of trucks, personnel carriers, and tanks. On one mission alone, Levi Chase destroyed eighty-four guns and some trucks and earned the nickname, "One Man Wave of Destruction." Chase had phenomenal eyesight. Once Cochran and the others were mystified when Chase peeled out of formation and howled down to line up his guns on a series of haystacks. But when Chase's .50 calibers opened up and the slugs tore into the stacks, they exploded. As Chase had detected, the hay was merely camouflage to hide ammunition stores.

Cochran's revitalized squadron became so efficient at interrupting enemy convoys that, as Cochran put it, "the Jerries and the Eyeties weren't able to move a truck anywhere in Tunisia by daylight." Once the squadron had been welded into a real fighting team, Cochran sent them after enemy aircraft as well. In one five-day period, the Red Scarf Guerrillas shot down thirty-four

The RAF made extensive use of American-made Bostons to harass the Afrika Korps. Fighters escorted this medium bomber on low sweeps behind German lines.

German and Italian aircraft, working the skies by day and by night. When Cochran left the desert to go to the China-Burma-India theater, he left behind a great fighter squadron able to carry on under a new commander. He had also become a legend in his time. Later, he would be immortalized in the comic strip *Terry and the Pirates* as "Flip Corkin."

Rommel's drive to capture the cities of Alexandria and Cairo came dangerously close to succeeding, but at the great tank and infantry battle of El Alamein, he was defeated by the British Eighth Army and thereafter the Afrika Korps was forced relentlessly back into Tunisia. The Germans were hit from one side by the British under Field Marshal Montgomery, and from the other side by the Americans under such generals as Eisenhower, Patton, and Bradley. Rommel's plight was made all the more desperate because he depended upon supplies and reinforcements to reach him from Italy and Sicily, and Allied air power was growing daily while that of the Luftwaffe dwindled. British and American bombers turned the Mediterranean Sea into a graveyard of sunken Axis ships, and Allied airpower destroyed almost everything that moved behind the German lines. The American 9th Air Force had joined with the 12th Air Force and the RAF to hammer ceaselessly at German and Italian troops who never seemed to be able to find cover from the murderous fighters that flew back and forth practically unopposed, their guns and cannons chewing to pieces anything on wheels.

New planes and new weapons were thrown into the battle by the combined Desert Air Forces. One of the most successful air weapons was the Hurricane IID "Hurribuster," or as they later were called, "Can Openers." Since the fighting in the desert had begun, fighter planes were used to strafe enemy tanks. But even .50-caliber and 20-mm shells could inflict only temporary damage on armored vehicles; what was needed was something with a heavier punch, something revolutionary. Hurricanes were modified with the installation of two Bofors 40-mm automatic cannon, weapons originally designed for antiaircraft use aboard ships and on the ground. These big guns were mounted, one to a wing, in pods with the barrels cleared to fire outside the arc of the propeller. Each gun weighed 320 pounds, which slowed the Hurricane, but that was of little importance. Each 40-mm shell weighed 2½ pounds, left the barrel at high velocity, and could penetrate all but the heaviest armor plate. The Hurribusters were shipped to Africa in the greatest

Nemesis of German tanks, trucks and armored cars was the Hurricane 11D, fitted with special 40-mm cannon under each wing. The recoil was brutal, but the effect on enemy transportation was far worse.

secrecy, and when they flew their first missions against Rommel's panzers, the Germans received the surprise of their lives; hundreds of tanks were left burning in the sands throughout Tunisia.

By the spring of 1943, the Afrika Korps and its Italian cohorts were penned up on the northern tip of Tunisia. With their backs to the sea, the Germans fought against the inevitable defeat. By this time Axis convoys were losing two out of three ships that attempted to bring supplies in, or troops out. All that was left to the Germans were air shuttles between Italy and Africa, using unwieldy Junkers–52 transports, tri-engined corrugated troop carriers that were slow and carried no armament. On a warm Sunday, late in April, American fighters created one of the greatest aerial slaughters in the history of warfare when a large force of Ju–52s were intercepted outbound over the calm blue of the Mediterranean.

Three squadrons of the U.S. 57th Fighter Group, nearly fifty P–40E Warhawks in all, were on patrol when one of the pilots saw approaching in the distance a monstrous formation of enemy planes. As the two forces drew closer, the spellbound American pilots counted approximately ninety of the lumbering Ju–52 transports, hugging the sea for protection, while above were numbers of Me–109s flying escort. Part of the P–40s climbed to keep the Messerschmitts busy, while the majority of the Warhawks charged their guns and waded into the mass of transports.

The excited Americans hardly knew which target to fasten onto first; everywhere they looked the big, gray vulnerable Junkers filled their sights. Many of the transports were laden with drums filled to the brim with diesel and high-octane fuel; these exploded in great fiery balls of shredded metal when the heavy .50-caliber slugs tore into their vitals. Others were loaded with ammunition, and these came apart spectacularly, tossing engines, framework, and crewmen into the sea. Others merely plunged heavily into the water, diving straight to the bottom. The elephantine transports lurched this way and that, jinking desperately to avoid the streams of machine-gun slugs that laced the sky, but there was no escape; it was as though a horde of insects had flown into a cloud of poison gas to die and tumble ungracefully to destruction.

The Me–109s tried desperately to protect their charges, but at low altitudes their greatest advantages of speed and agility were gone, and the P–40s enjoyed

Workhorse of the Luftwaffe was the Ju–52 transport, used to ferry troops, ammunition and fuel to Rommel's hard-pressed men in the dessert. Slow and unarmed, the Ju–52 was easy prey for American and RAF fighters who shot them down by the dozens.

a field day with the enemy fighters as well: sixteen Me–109s were shot down, and the Americans lost six.

The battle continued until the remnants of transport formation reached the shores of Tunisia, where the shattered pilots set the big planes down anywhere to get away from the buzzsaw American fighters. Two-thirds of the transports were shot out of the sky in a furious ten minutes of shooting-gallery combat that sealed the doom of the Germans in Africa. Sixty out of ninety planes blown to pieces. No more, ordered Hitler, no more.

On May 3, 1943, the final ground assault in Tunisia began. The Germans, exhausted and denied supplies, fought back with their usual skills and bravery, but on May 7, the U.S. II Corps captured the town of Bizerte, and the British entered the city of Tunis. On May 13, the last Axis fighting man laid down his arms, to join 275,000 other prisoners inside barbed-wire cages that stretched for acres.

The way was open for the invasion of "the soft underbelly," and in Germany, where he had flown before the final collapse, Field Marshal Erwin Rommel had second thoughts about the value of air power.

But of course the thoughts came much too late.

Heavy losses by day forced the Germans to begin night operations against England using such black-painted bombers as the Do–215.

6/COMBAT BY MOONLIGHT

ALTHOUGH THE BATTLE of Britain had been won and there was no longer a real threat of invasion after the end of September 1940, the ordeal of the English people was not over. The Luftwaffe, defeated by daylight, began coming under cover of darkness. Raids lashed the island every night during the winter when weather permitted, and with the coming of spring and clearer skies the full weight of Goering's night raiders was brought to bear from one end of England to the other. The coastal town of Plymouth was bombed five nights out of seven during the latter part of April. More than 600 civilians were killed and 20,000 homes were destroyed. London remained the primary target throughout the night blitz, and in that same month the city shook with the rain of high explosives dropped from German bombers flying in formations 450 strong. On the night of May 10, a night that seemed to last forever to those in the burning city, nearly 1,500 Londoners lost their lives in the cataclysm of flames, blast waves, falling buildings, and flying steel.

When the massive night raids began, the RAF was poorly prepared to fight in the dark. The principle of airborne radar was known, but the necessary miniaturization in order to fit one of the "black boxes" inside an aircraft had not yet been accomplished. Defensive measures born of desperation were resorted to in an attempt to bring down the German marauders. Planes were loaded with searchlights and sent into the sky to throw a powerful beam against enemy bombers in order that the British night fighters could see what they were shooting at. Other bombers were sent aloft to drop parachute mines, hoping that Heinkels would run into them as they floated slowly earthwards. Magnesium flares were scattered over target cities so that the defending fighter pilots might pick out raiders and shoot them down. But these devices posed as much threat to the fighters as they did to the bombers,

Spitfires in nighttime colors were effective against German raiders even without radar to guide them to target. Bright moonlight often provided Spitfire pilots brilliant silhouettes of Luftwaffe bombers.

and were quickly junked—along with such suggestions from the public as scattering sand into the sky and thus fouling the Germans' engines. Until the first of the airborne radar units became operational, the British night interceptors were forced to grope in the dark, using only their eyeballs coupled with less-than-pinpoint guidance from the ground.

Despite the primitive conditions, Fighter Command's night-flying Spitfires and Hurricanes achieved great success in shooting down, on an average, twenty or more bombers each night. Fighter patrols were kept aloft throughout the hours of darkness, waiting to be vectored to the vicinity of enemy forces by Ground Intercept Stations who watched the approach of bombers on small radar screens. Not infrequently, fighter pilots managed to spot inbound or outbound raiders on their own. There were a number of tricks night-fighter pilots used to overcome the handicap of darkness. They wore red goggles, or stayed in dimly lighted rooms prior to scheduled takeoffs in order to preserve night vision. They learned to scan the inky sky with the corners of their eyes, where night vision is most acute. They drank a great deal of carrot juice, which many believed was an aid to seeing in the dark. Some flew with their canopies open, accepting the icy blast of wind in trade for unobstructed vision. These procedures paid handsome dividends for a young pilot officer named Andrew Humphrey, of 266 Squadron, who achieved spectacular results on night patrol during the height of the night-time blitz.

Humphrey was patrolling at 18,000 feet over Nottingham when out of the corner of his eye he saw thin, ghostly vapor trails 2,000 feet above his Spitfire. Humphrey put on throttle and started climbing. He made out the smudgy outlines of a Heinkel 111, heading for the Channel. The Germans saw the Spitfire just as Humphrey started closing the range, and the pilot started diving, hoping to reach a friendly field before the Britisher's guns could do their work. The crucial game of follow-the-leader swept downward through the darkness until the Heinkel reached the Belgian coast. The Spitfire was now at 3,000 feet altitude and on the tail of the He-111, whose flickering blue exhausts loomed large in Humphrey's sights. He pressed his thumb on the firing button and tracers from the eight Brownings leapt out, seeming to connect the two airplanes with fiery lines. The bomber exploded in a mushrooming ball of orange fire, blinding Humphrey, who racked his Spitfire around in a hard turn to avoid flying into the flaming debris.

When Humphrey recovered his night vision, he looked downward to orient himself with the ground and discovered that he was directly above a German bomber base then launching a fresh wave of attackers bound for England. He reefed the Spitfire around in a diving turn, leveling out immediately above the deck and directly astern of an He-111 just getting airborne. Humphrey flew so close to the bomber before he opened fire that he nearly rammed the big enemy machine, and when the Heinkel burst into flames and cartwheeled downward it was all Humphrey could do to avoid colliding with the falling bomber. He jerked the Spit upwards to get away from the tracered flak pouring at him from the ground—and found himself in the same sky with a prowling Me-110. Humphrey bounced the twin-engined fighter, but his ammunition ran out after only a short burst. The Me-110 disappeared, and Humphrey, low on fuel and far from home, decided to call it a night.

One of the handsomest aircraft produced during the war had disappointed its designers and terrified its crew when it was sent into combat to perform its intended role of day interceptor, but it came into its own over Britain when the night raids began.

The Boulton Paul Defiant I was a two-seater fighter, unusual in that it carried no guns firing forward. Instead, the Defiant's punch was carried in a power turret just aft of the pilot, a turret mounting quadruple .303 Browning machine guns. The theory was that the pilot, unhampered by having to think about gunnery, would better be able to fly the aircraft into killing position, where the gunner, unhampered by having to think about piloting, could concentrate his energies on pure marksmanship. Unfortunately, as is so often the case, brilliant theories often prove disastrous when put to the test, and the Defiants proved to be sitting game for Me–109s in air-to-air combat. Only once or twice did the Defiant raise false hopes inside Fighter Command. During the raid on Dieppe, a Defiant squadron managed to shoot down a number of German fighters whose pilots mistook the unfamiliar Defiants for Hurricanes and made firing passes from above and to the rear. The surprised Germans ran into a storm of fire from the waiting turret gunner and were blown apart before they could realize their mistake. But the word quickly spread, and once the German pilots learned that the Defiants were totally harmless from the front they could take their time in fastening their sights on the hapless planes' blind spot, behind and below, and massacred them. The Defiants' top speed was only 304 mph and they could neither run away nor offer effective combat. During one disastrous encounter in the fall of 1940, five out of seven Defiants were shot down one after the other, and shortly afterward they were forbidden further action by day.

The remaining Defiants were painted black, fitted with flame-damping devices on the exhaust ports, and distributed among ten RAF squadrons to fight by night. Now the Defiant's great qualities as a well-mannered, stable

Boulton-Paul Defiants were hopeless as RAF daytime fighters, but proved effective against German nighttime marauders.

First radar-equipped British night fighter to see heavy action in England's moonlit skies was the two-seater, twin-engined Bristol Beaufighter.

gun platform began to pay dividends. The pilot could concentrate on flying so that his gunner would be in position in the enemy's blind spot, and once there the Defiant could be held steady while the gunner lashed enemy bombers with a concentration of lead, sometimes with the four gun barrels pointing nearly straight up to tear gaping holes in the bellies of the He–111s.

However it was an altogether new kind of night fighter that the Germans dreaded most. The Bristol Beaufighter I was introduced into the night skies over England during the winter of 1940, and Luftwaffe casualties rose. The Beaufighter was a big, powerful, front-heavy machine powered with twin 1,590-hp Bristol Hercules XI engines enabling the ten-ton fighter to climb at 1,850 feet per minute, reaching a top speed of 323 mph. The Beaufighter was awesomely armed, carrying four closely spaced 20-mm cannons in the nose and six .303-caliber machine guns in the wings.

Along with the new Beaufighter was introduced the Mark IV A.I. (for Air Intercept) radar complex mounted in a special compartment aft of the pilot. The Mk–IV could pick up radar returns at a maximum distance of four miles, its minimum capability was 600 feet, and it went a long way toward bringing about the demise of the German bombers over England. Manning the radar sets in Beaufighters were ex-gunners with special training in operating the "Thing," as it sometimes was called, and during night interception missions they were some of the busiest men in the air.

The radar man sat in an elevated metal seat behind the pilot, his head poking up inside a plastic dome that afforded good visibility foreward and aft. The Thing, a little black metal box, was suspended from the roof just behind the dome. Once contact was made with an enemy bomber, the operator sat with his forehead pressed against an oval rubber shield, his eyes glued on the greenish blips flickering on the small radar screen. The blips told him the bearing and approximate distance to the target, and this information was relayed to the pilot in the directional commands; whether to climb, descend, turn right or left. Once the pilot was in visual contact with the target, the radar operator swiveled around to prepare for the violent action to follow. When the four Hispano cannons opened up, the noise inside the Beaufighter was deafening and the interior of the fuselage came alive with lurid blue and orange flames sweeping back from the guns. The cannons ran through a full load of 240 rounds very quickly, then the radar man had to drop down from his lofty perch and struggle with the sixty-pound drums of fresh ammunition, heaving them forward and trying not to mash his fingers while he wrestled the heavy cans into place above the breech blocks. If the pilot was turning the Beaufighter, trying to stick to his quarry's tail, the job was made enormously complicated by the added G-load, and if

The Wooden Wonder, a British DeHavilland Mosquito, was one of the most versatile fighters ever made. Mosquitos with advanced radar could catch and kill any night intruder the Germans had to offer.

the plane was flying through turbulent air, it was all the loader could do to keep his feet while encumbered with the awkward cans.

Because the destruction of the laden German bombers was usually executed at close range, sometimes at less than 100 yards, the experience was searing and unforgettable to Beaufighter crews. Once the guns were zeroed squarely and started their deadly pounding, enemy bombers simply came apart in the air. Almost always the fuel tanks exploded, and there was no way, as a rule, that the Beaufighter pilot could avoid flying through some part of the debris. The destroyer plane bounced wildly in the turbulence, but worst of all was the nauseating stench of burning metal alloy and paint that penetrated the crew's oxygen masks to linger in nostrils long after the mission was over. Men, too, were burning in those planes that fell through space like a thrown torch eerily illuminating the clouds with a ghostly translucence.

Massed raids by night on England tapered off during the early summer of 1941 as Hitler prepared to attack Russia. The bulk of the Luftwaffe was transferred to the Eastern Front, relieving the pressure on the people of Britain. German bombers and bomb-carrying fighters made hit-and-run raids from across the Channel, but sustained heavy casualties in doing so. In the fall of 1942, Fighter Command received a brand-new day-and-night-fighter that easily outclassed any German bomber made. The De Havilland Mosquito was unique in World War II, being the only all-wood combat airplane manufactured. The "Wooden Wonder," as it was called, carried a crew of two, was armed with four 20-mm cannon, and its twin Merlin engines gave

Heavy British raids on German cities forced German fighter pilots to take to darkened skies in an attempt to halt the destruction. This Me–110 was fitted with special radar gear, including cumbersome antennae fixed to nose.

the lightweight fighter a top speed of 425 mph. The combined power of 3,240 horses working with the broad-surfaced wings enabled the Mosquito to climb above 36,000 feet, and special pressurized versions could get nearly ten miles above the earth, high enough to discourage even the special models of the versatile Ju–88s that flew at extreme altitudes to observe, or to bomb.

In 1942, the RAF began the great terror raids over Germany. The giant Lancasters, Halifaxes, and Stirlings went out long after the sun went down, strung across the Channel and into Germany in one long river of destruction. Where Goering could put up 450 medium bombers over London, Sir Arthur "Bomber" Harris massed 1,000 heavies and sent them against such densely populated towns as Cologne, Hamburg, Essen, Lübeck and Düsseldorf. The four-engined bombers were loaded with two-, four- and six-ton "block-busters." Others rained down incendiaries. Cities were blown apart and gutted by firestorms of historic intensity. People died by the tens of thousands below, and by the hundreds above.

The Germans defended their airspace with tenacity, with skill, and with bravery. Pilots of Bomber Command learned what it meant to fly through the heaviest concentration of flak in the world and what it was like to have to grimly maintain close formation in darkened skies filled with bomber-hunting Me–110s and Ju–88s equipped with superior radar.

The new German radar, known as the Lichtenstein radar, presented to the operator, information on three separate tubes so that he could get an accurate fix on enemy bombers regarding altitude, distance and bearing. Elaborate forklike antennae were fitted to the noses of the Junkers and Messerschmitts equipped for night-fighting operations, and these antennae swept a field thirty degrees above and below the plane's nose and sixty degrees to the right and left. The range of the Lichtenstein radar corresponded to the height above the ground. Thus if an Me–110 was maintaining an altitude of 15,000 feet, the radar could "acquire" a target that was just under three miles distant.

One of the great German night-interceptor pilots was *Oberleutnant* Rheinhold Knacke, twenty-four, who shot down forty-three British heavies while piloting a radar-equipped Me–110. Over Holland one night, Knacke's radar put him within less than 100 yards of a bomber headed for Germany, but his own plane was knocked out of the sky in a bizarre incident demonstrating the close-in nature of night combats over Europe.

Knacke was so close to the rear of the bomber, and the sky was so bright with moonlight, that he could see the British rear gunner huddled in his turret. When Knacke opened fire the gunner, either a very new and inexperienced airman or a veteran whose nerves were frayed by combat, simply abandond his turret, kicking away the escape hatch to tumble through space at 200 mph. His spinning body impacted against one of the night-fighter's engines and then disappeared. The damaged propeller vibrated so badly that the German pilot was forced to switch it off and return to base. The cowling and nose of the strangely downed fighter was quickly hosed off, but Knacke was out of combat until a new prop could be installed. Not long afterwards Knacke was killed by a rear-turret gunner of a Handley-Page Halifax who kept pouring fire into Knacke's Me–110 even after his own plane was burning and headed downward to crash on German soil.

The bitter contest for supremacy of the night skies over Germany continued throughout 1943 and 1944. Bomber Command was willing to accept five percent casualties out of any raiding force, but as German radar and Ground Control Intercept stations became more effective the casualty rate jumped to as high as eight and ten percent. Once the rate was even higher: 94 British heavy bombers were shot down during a raid on Nuremberg staged by fewer than 800 heavies, and another 70 returned home with dead or wounded crewmen aboard. Bomber pilots had to contend not only with radar-equipped fighters but with single-engined Me–109s and FW–190s that flew *inside* the bomber streams as they fought their way to and from the target cities. German fighter pilots often flew in their own flak in order to get within killing range of the bombers.

Eventually, the losses to Bomber Command became so severe that raids had to be confined to shorter-range targets inside Germany so that they could have night-fighter escorts whose range largely determined the operating radius of the bombers.

The entire picture of the war began to change when the U.S. Eighth Air Force arrived in England in numbers sufficient to inaugurate around-the-clock bombing of German cities and industrial targets.

Now the Luftwaffe had to contend not only with brave bomber crews who flew by day and night, but with a new breed of fighters that could fly very far indeed; all the way to Berlin and back, as Hermann Goering was to discover.

73

Big Friend, Little Friends. High-flying B–17 of 381st Bomb Group sees plenty of protection coming its way as four P–38s cross bomber formation to take up escort station.

7/BIG FRIEND, LITTLE FRIEND

THE UNITED STATES was plunged into war with Germany on December 11, 1941, and as in 1918, the nation was almost totally unprepared. But military planners had faith that the British could continue to hold the enemy at bay until American industry could gear up for total war, until a huge army could be raised and trained, and until the phrase, "U.S. air power," could take on real meaning. The planners realized that ultimate victory in Europe would require invasion of the Continent, but first aerial supremacy must be won. German industry must be crippled by precision daylight bombing, its warmaking capacity destroyed.

The British, who had already been fighting an air war with Germany for twenty-seven months, flatly told the Americans that their plan to bomb Germany by daylight was suicidal. The RAF, and the Luftwaffe before them, had discovered to their cost that only under the cover of darkness could bomber formations attack Germany with acceptable losses. The Americans pointed out that whereas the Luftwaffe's medium bombers were skimpily armed, the big four-engined B–17 Flying Fortress and B–24 Liberators carried ten .50-caliber machine guns firing all around the clock and that carefully worked out formations would enable the gunners to offer interlocking fire to German fighters, no matter what direction they attacked from. Moreover, new American fighters on the way would be able to escort their Big Friends deep inside Germany and return.

The question was, when? When would American air power be brought to bear? When would the hundreds, then thousands, of U.S. bombers and fighters arrive in the United Kingdom to team with the RAF and begin to deal death blows to Germany on an around-the-clock basis?

It wasn't until seven months after America entered the war that American airmen in U.S. uniforms bombed German targets. On July 4, 1942, the men of the 15th Bombardment Squadron celebrated Independence Day by bombing Luftwaffe airfields in Holland, but they had to borrow Douglas A–20 twin-engine bombers from the RAF to make the gesture. More than a month passed before the American Eighth Bomber Command could get into action using its own aircraft. On August 17, a dozen B–17s of the 97th Bomb Group raided the railway yards at Rouen-Sotteville in France. The first B–17s lost to enemy action were shot down by German fighters on September 6 in a strike at the Potez aircraft factory at Meaulte. Then, finally, on January 27, 1943—more than twelve months after entering the war—the U.S. Army Air Forces struck at Germany: the 1st Bomb Wing, Eighth Air Force, attacked Wilhelmshaven and Emden, and the great struggle for the skies over the enemy heartland was on.

The first of the promised fighters to arrive in the United Kingdom were Republic P–47C Thunderbolts, the largest, heaviest, piston-engine single-seat fighter ever built. The maximum gross weight of the Thunderbolt was 14,925 pounds. Pilots of the 4th Fighter Group, most of whom were ex-Eagle Squadron members, gazed with dismay at the Thunderbolt the first time they saw it; it looked exactly like a milk bottle on legs, and was quickly christened the "Jug." The big, squat fighter weighed more than twice as much as the racy-looking Spitfire. Its massive cowling housed an 18-cylinder Pratt & Whitney engine that developed 2,300-hp, and its broad wings enclosed eight .50-caliber guns. A heavy fighter such as this one could not be expected to climb quickly, and it couldn't; it took the Jug more than seven minutes to get to 15,000 feet. But the P–47 had its advantages. It could top 425 mph at 27,000 feet and it could outdive either Me–109s or FW–190s, which was a decided advantage in combat if the outmaneuvered pilot wanted to break away. There were two other features about the Jug that pilots liked: the roomy cockpit and the fact that the plane looked as if it could absorb heavy battle damage and still keep flying, like a battleship with wings. Early P–47s had a limited range of only 640 miles, which meant that they could escort the bombers only so far over the continent, but in the summer of 1943 range was upped to 1,250 miles with the addition of drop tanks. Later Thunderbolts arriving in England, the P–47Ds, had a range of 1,800 miles, enough to fly nonstop from London to Moscow.

Drawing upon the experience of RAF fighter pilots, including such aces as Johnny Johnson and Douglas Bader (who flew Spitfires in combat despite the fact that he wore aluminum legs,) the Americans adopted the standard "finger four" formation when flying missions over enemy territory. The RAF had learned long ago that the line-astern and the classic Vee of Vees formations were totally useless as tactical combat formations. If you spread your hand, tucking the thumb under the palm, and imagine a fighter plane at each finger tip, you will have a perfect description of the finger-four formation used by World War II fighter pilots. Each section of four aircraft was made up of two teams, the leader and his all-important wingman. The job of the wingman was to stick with his leader, flying just above and behind

Ground level view of P–47 reveals why these chunky fighters were affectionally called "Jugs" by the men who flew them. Droppable belly tanks gave Jugs greatly increased range. Stripes under wings and around fuselage were added just prior to D-Day, 1944, so that over-anxious ships' gunners and others would not mistake allied aircraft for those of the enemy.

Mustangs of 361st Fighter Group in close finger-four formation.

Johnny Godfrey (left) and Don Gentile, famed pilots of 4th Fighter Group, destroyed thirty-six German fighters in aerial combat between them. Godfrey and Gentile demonstrated that precision teamwork won battles and was a key to survival. "What he misses," commented Gentile, "I get."

Con trails over Germany. These Boeing B–17 Flying Fortresses weave fantastic patterns at high altitude. Although beautiful to the eye, condensation trails provided Germans with markers, made their task easier.

the leader's tail, so as to protect the leader and to provide the second half of a one-two punch in coordinated attacks on German fighters.

The outstanding fighter team of the war was made up of Don Gentile and John T. Godfrey, who flew with 336 Squadron of the 4th Fighter Group. Like Gentile, Godfrey had been trained by the RAF, but fate had kept him out of combat until the fall of 1943, when he had more than 400 hours of flying time in his logbooks. Godfrey's impatience to come to grips with the Germans after so long a wait got him into trouble with the 4th's CO, Colonel Chesley Peterson, and his rashness almost cost him his life as well.

On December 22, 1943, the 4th Group escorted B–17s to Münster. The English countryside shook with the massed roar of the Fortress engines as they departed one by one, squadron by squadron, group by group, to form up in combat boxes over Hertfordshire and then, tightly locked in a formation nearly two miles long and more than a mile deep, the Fortresses began marching across the Channel.

At Debden, thirty-five miles north of the heart of London, sixty-four Thunderbolts of the 4th Group roar off the runways in series to form their own formations and head out for Germany. The Thunderbolts climb up through thin clouds until they reach 30,000 feet. Flying more than twice as fast as the big silver Forts, they reach the rendezvous area over the Belgian coast in plenty of time. Colonel Peterson fans the P–47s out until they are finger-foured in a covering blanket in front of, over, and behind the Big Friends plowing majestically through the sky.

Godfrey's section is in position behind the rear box of Fortresses and holding 8,000 feet of altitude above them. Then Godfrey, whose eyes were described as "perhaps the keenest in the Air Force," spots a pair of Me–109s cruising at the tail end of the trailing B–17s, their pilots apparently trying to make up their minds about attacking so many guns, or acting as decoys for more Me–109s hidden in the sun. They seem to be just sitting there, inviting trouble. Godfrey can't stand it; he calls out that he is attacking. Then he pushes the stick forward and the heavy Thunderbolt drops like a keg of nails through the sky. The altimeter unwinds as the air speed indicator needle keeps pace, indicating more than 500 mph. The mile and a half of space separating the P–47 from the 109s is quickly eaten up. Godfrey levels out behind the Me–109s without being seen. He lines up the lead ship in his reflective sights and jams his thumb against the firing button. The eight .50 calibers begin chugging, the Thunderbolt slows with the recoil, and Godfrey sees the fireflylike strikes all over the Messerschmitt. Parts of the plane are ripped away and the engine begins belching smoke. Godfrey eases the stick over and watches his tracers stitch holes in the second plane. The German pilot blows his canopy, stands up with his hand on the ripcord and goes over the side. Two kills in less than a minute! Godfrey is elated.

"Break, Purple Two, Break!"

The urgent cry in Godfrey's headset jerks him out of his state of giddiness. Far above, the other P–47 pilots had seen Godfrey's kills, and they had seen a third Me–109 come from nowhere to climb on Godfrey's tail. Cannon shells tore into Godfrey's P–47. He felt the impact as they ripped through his wings and his spine was jarred as one exploded against the armor plate at his back. Fiery red streaks were passing on both sides of the canopy. Godfrey jammed the stick back against his stomach and shoved hard on the left rudder pedal. The violent maneuver that followed caused the big Thunder-bolt to tumble in the sky, and the Me–109 streaked past, still firing into empty air. One of the P–47s that had joined in the melee shot the Me–109 down.

Godfrey spun away, recovering from the wild gyrations only 4,000 feet above the earth. He pulled out with such force that he blacked out, and when he recovered he did not know where he was. His radio was shot to pieces and the instrument panel riddled with shrapnel. He climbed back to 15,000 feet to get his bearings. There, in an empty sky, he recovered his wits and turned on the proper compass heading for home, hoping that the Jug would stay together. The controls felt mushy, and Godfrey realized that he could not afford further combat. He pushed the nose over and leveled out right on the deck, streaking over the Belgian countryside, dodging flak as he reached the coast and the Channel, whose white-topped waves were only inches from the tips of the whirling propeller blades. With the fuel needle sagging on Empty, Godfrey put the crippled Jug down at the nearest RAF fighter base. He cut the switches, weakly pushed back the canopy, crawled from the cockpit and eased himself onto the grass—and immediately threw up. His hands shook so badly that an RAF officer had to light his cigarette for him and put it between his lips. Later, with most of the fright and queasiness gone, Godfrey had the P–47 refueled and he flew back to Debden a wiser man.

The idea went home that teamwork was required not only to beat the enemy fighters, but to survive. Thereafter Godfrey, as Gentile's wingman, stuck close. Together, as though they were a left and a right mailed fist directed with a single brain, they began to shoot down Germans and to bring their Jugs home in one piece. Gentile discovered just how valuable his wingman was during a fighter sweep in the Paris area shortly before the end of 1943.

Gentile spotted a gaggle of fifteen FW–190s flying east, some 5,000 feet beneath the squadron of P–47s he was leading. He called out the sighting, then told Godfrey he was going down. The Hun fighters were "bounced" unawares, and as they broke apart to give combat Gentile and Godfrey separated two of the 190s and went after them, Gentile's Thunderbolt in the lead.

The German pilots saw that they were under attack and immediately threw their FW–190s in hard banks, heeled around, leveled out in tight 180-degree turns and came straight at the Americans. The four fighters barreled at each other at a closure rate of more than 700 mph. Gentile set his teeth, determined not to be first to break. The round noses and thin wings of the enemy fighters loomed closer and closer, but Gentile bored on through the sky. Then the Germans broke at the last split second. "They broke together," said Gentile, "and I knew they were afraid of me and that I was going to kill them." The Focke-Wulfs flopped on their backs and dived straight for the deck. Gentile rolled and went after them, his gloved finger toying with the firing button. He did not bother to call to see if Godfrey was still with him. Why should he? Godfrey was *always* there. Except this time Godfrey was not: when the FWs headed for the deck Godfrey was bounced by two more fighters, and he had turned in to them to break up their attack, keeping from Gentile's unprotected rear.

Nothing would dive as fast as the Thunderbolt, and Gentile caught up with the fleeing FW–190s and shot them both down over the forest of Compiègne. Gentile watched them crash into the green woods, then hauled back on the stick to get altitude. He discovered not Godfrey, but two experienced German pilots on his tail. They were so close that he could make out the details of their helmets and oxygen masks. Then he watched as the noses and the wings of the Focke-Wulfs became sheeted with flame. Cannon shells and machine-gun bullets ripped into his Thunderbolt. Gaping holes appeared in his starboard wing. Gentile snapped out of his trance and almost

The Luftwaffe's finest fighter was the Focke–Wulf 190, a speedy radial-engined interceptor and duelist capable of near 400 mph speeds and blessed with a high rate of climb.

violently horsed the stick back and over, turning in to the attacking Germans, determined to ram the leader. The enemy pilot jumped his 190 over the American P–47 and flashed past. Gentile nudged stick and rudder and headed for the trailing FW–190, but the German panicked and broke away and out of the fight. Gentile followed, spraying the sky with lead, but the German got away when Gentile's guns sputtered to a stop one after the other.

Now the first FW was back on Gentile's tail, and firing while Gentile was still in a turn. Tracers flashed past the American fighter and Gentile broke out in a sweat all over again. He tightened his turn and watched the stream of cannon shells fly past his nose only forty feet away. The German, Gentile realized, was "a hard man who knew the tricks of the trade." An FW could turn inside a P–47, and slowly the stream of lead began to inch back toward Gentile's P–47. All Gentile could do was to keep turning hard, offering the German angled shots, and hoping he would not fly into the ground.

The combat raged from 50 to 100 feet above the trees of Compiègne. Gentile's plane suddenly flicked over on its back and he watched the green leaves fly past his head upside down. The German was still there, still firing. Gentile timed his recovery so that he came out of his inverted attitude flying alongside the surprised Focke-Wulf pilot. Gentile scrabbled for words to call out to his wondering friends in the other P–47s still milling around in combat somewhere over Paris. "Help! Help!" he screamed into his mike. "I'm being clobbered!"

"Where are you, Don?" somebody called back. All Gentile could say was that he saw a railroad track nearby. The German pilot was pulling away from the strange two-ship formation, getting ready to attack again, and Gentile had no time to give precise directions. The German came on again, firing, and Gentile turned in to him head-on, offering only a second or two in which the German could keep his sights on the P–47. Gentile kept his head; a less experienced pilot would have broken and fled for home, but Gentile knew that the veteran pilot and his FW–190—now in front of him, now behind him, now flashing past him—would quickly close in for the kill once the P–47 turned tail to run.

The bizarre duel roared on for fifteen minutes. The crafty German would not give an inch and neither would Gentile. The unequal fight ended only when the German exhausted his ammunition and headed home. Gentile flew back to Debden on the dregs of his fuel supply, happy enough, as he said later, to get out on a cloud and dance on it.

One destroyed. An Me–109 goes down in flames, victim of P–47 guns.

One of the 4th Group pilots, Lieutenant Jack Raphael, composed a song in honor of Gentile's experience, and on squadron party nights Gentile had to endure the words, accompanied by a piano to the tune of "Tramp, Tramp, Tramp, the Boys are Marching."

> Help, help, help! I'm being clobbered,
> Down here by the railroad track.
> Two 190s chase me around,
> And we're damn near to the ground,
> Tell them I got two if I don't make it back.

Gentile, who would go on to receive confirmation for twenty-three air-to-air kills, said of the fight over Compiègne forest that it was the most critical he had ever fought because "it showed me what I had learned and it taught me what I was." The combat had taxed Gentile to the limit, and he had survived.

The new year, 1944, ushered in significant changes to the 4th Fighter Group. Colonel Peterson was replaced as CO by Colonel Donald Blakeslee, another ex-Eagle, and a square-jawed, hardboiled commander who made things clear to the pilots of the 4th the day he arrived at Debden. Blakeslee told the pilots that the 4th was going to be the best fighter outfit in the European Theater of Operations. They would all fly hard and fight hard, and if anybody there didn't want to meet his standards he could transfer out right now. Blakeslee was only twenty-six, but he already had racked up more hours in the air than anybody else in the group.

Blakeslee then managed to reequip his group with the new North American P-51D Mustang fighters that had recently arrived in England. To get them, Blakeslee had to promise the Chief of Eighth Air Force Fighter Command, General William Kepner, that the 4th Fighter Group would transition into the Mustangs within twenty-four hours. He flew a P-51 back to Debden, and the pilots took turns at the controls, each allowed only forty minutes in the air. Then the entire group flew their P-47s to Steeple Morten, parked them, climbed into factory-fresh P-51s and took off on a fighter sweep over France, learning to handle the new fighter on the way.

The pilots were wildly enthusiastic over their new Mustangs. Much smaller than the Jug, the P-51 weighed only 10,100 pounds fully loaded, could climb to 10,000 feet in just over three minutes, and its 1,695-hp Merlin engine pushed the fighter to 437 mph. The pilots discovered that the P-51 could turn with either Me-109s or FW-190s; they now could duel success-fully with the Germans at any altitude up to nearly 40,000 feet. And the range of the P-51 was fantastic. Fitted with drop tanks, the P-51 had a range of 2,080 miles, more than any other fighter.

On March 3, 1944, the new Mustangs proved their worth in the first fighter sweep over Berlin. Sixteen P-51s left Debden to escort B-17s to the German capital, but eight were forced to abort because of engine trouble. The other eight swept on across Germany in poor weather, not hearing the recall order given to the Fortresses. The speeding Mustangs broke through scattered clouds over Berlin vainly seeking their Big Friends. They found instead approximately sixty German fighters, Me–109s, FW–190s, Me–210s and even a handful of Do–17s sent up to protect the capital. The P–51s blundered into this enemy armada and were quickly surrounded. The Germans poured down on the astonished Americans and the sky seemed to them to be filled with nothing but black-crossed wings and tightly woven webs of tracers. Major Gilbert Halsley, leading, cried, "Let's get out of here!"

The Mustangs somehow managed to avoid annihilation, losing three out of the eight fighters as they clawed their way through the mass of German planes. Gentile not only escaped unharmed, but raised his score to ten by bagging a pair of FW–190s.

Five days later, on March 8, the 4th Group returned to Berlin and took vengeance. The Mustangs joined battle with the German fighters at a moment when the skies over Berlin were filled with smoke from B–17s and Me–109s going down, with the ugly black clusters of bombs falling and with white blossoms of parachute silk. The Big Friends were having a hard time, and Godfrey and Gentile waded into the melee with blazing guns.

Godfrey stayed glued to Gentile's tail while Gentile blew an Me–109 apart. Then Godfrey assumed the lead and called for Gentile to fly his wing while he broke to the right to bounce another Me–109 that was attacking a straggling Fortress. Godfrey's six guns hammered the enemy fighter to shreds and it flopped over and went down trailing a thick plume of black smoke. The Mustangs climbed to 28,000 feet, above the swarm of German fighters. Gentile saw two Me–109s separate from the rest and begin turning to press their attack on outlying B–17s. Gentile called, "You take the one on the right and I'll get the one on the left." The P–51s nosed over and sliced down on the Germans.

The Me–109s stupidly flew straight ahead and the two Americans leveled out directly astern of the enemy fighters and opened fire simultaneously. A two-second burst was all it took; one Me rolled over to the right and went down, the other rolled to the left and twisted through the clouds on fire.

Godfrey looked over his right shoulder and saw a single 109 diving. He called, "Six o'clock high, a single bandit."

"Okay," Gentile replied, "you break right and I'll break left."

The Mustangs flew on, seemingly unsuspecting. The German pilot kept coming, closer, closer.

"Break!"

Leader of the 4th Fighter Group, Colonel Don Blakeslee, seen in the cockpit of P–51D Mustang.

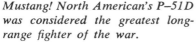

Mustang! North American's P–51D was considered the greatest long-range fighter of the war.

Mustang fighter pilot, Lieutenant Bill Groseclose, climbs into snug cockpit prior to takeoff and rendezvous with bombers.

The two Mustangs split apart, and the German turned with Godfrey and opened fire. Godfrey tightened his turn, keeping the tracers running ahead of his nose. Gentile completed his turn and came at the German head-on. The German broke and rolled underneath Gentile's Mustang. Gentile rolled after him and went down, firing. Godfrey resumed his wingman's position and added his own guns to Gentile's. They could see strikes all over the German fighter, but the pilot would not bail out or quit the fight. He put the Me–109 into a split-S and came back for Gentile with his guns working. Godfrey hammered him some more, then his ammo ran out. He told Gentile.

"Okay, I'll finish him," Gentile replied.

He rolled away from the German's fire and turned hard and got back on the Me–109's tail. The German half-rolled and went for the deck in a maneuver that often worked when attacked by Spitfires. But the Mustang could dive just as fast as an Me–109 and Gentile closed the range quickly. His guns chugged again and Gentile watched glycol stream back from the damaged German fighter. With his engine starting to overheat, the German decided to save his life. They were directly over Berlin, so close to the streets that Gentile could count bricks. The German pulled up sharply, blew his canopy off and hit the silk at only 1,000 feet. Gentile watched as the Me–109 plowed into a city street and disintegrated.

In twenty minutes over Berlin, Gentile and Godfrey destroyed six German fighters. On the way back to Debden they picked up a lone Fortress, straggling behind the rest. The P–51s approached the B–17 slowly, not wishing to be mistaken for FW–190s or Me–109s. Then they started weaving back and forth above the bomber until they were sure the Fortress gunners—who tended to shoot first and identify the victims later—recognized them as Little Friends. Godfrey dropped down and flew alongside the B–17. Part of the crew was crowded at the starboard waist gun position, blowing kisses at him.

In June 1944, Gentile and Godfrey were pulled out of combat and sent back to the United States where they were given a hero's welcome, then sent on tour to make speeches and encourage the people at home to buy more War Bonds. Gentile was kept in the States, but Godfrey managed to be returned to combat in August. Godfrey's one ambition was to become the top-ranking ace, and he had set himself a goal of fifty destroyed before retiring from the high arena over Germany. Including aircraft destroyed on the ground, Godfrey's score stood at twenty-six.

The invasion of France was nearly sixty days old when Godfrey returned to combat, but the Germans were fighting as fiercely as ever. Targets were plentiful. On August 5, Godfrey and his wingmate flew a free-lance mission

Eighth Air Force armorers carry .50 caliber machine guns and belt-loaded ammunition to waiting P–51. Total rounds seen here were used to feed one gun only.

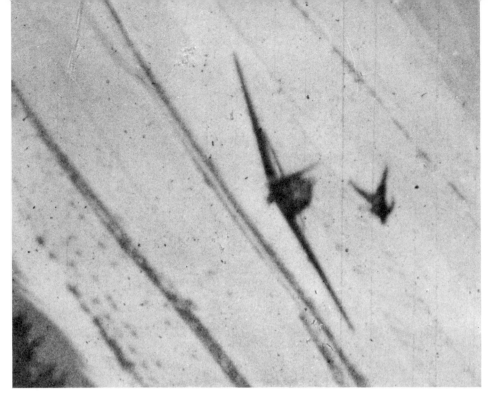

Bail out! Major James Dalglish, Thunderbolt pilot, recorded this dramatic scene with 16-mm gun camera after riddling FW–190 with machine gun fire. German pilot flies through space before popping parachute.

on a sweep over Germany and returned home after destroying eight loco-motives, three Ju–52s parked on an airfield, and an Me–109 caught napping near the ground. To make sure his kills were confirmed, Godfrey wheeled around and flew down into the flak in order to make a 16-mm film record of the burning Junkers. Back at Debden, Godfrey was shocked to see that the underside of his P–51 was scorched and riddled with small holes from flaming debris thrown up during his low-level strafing runs.

The next day Godfrey bagged a twin-engine Me–110 flying at 2,000 feet thirty miles east of Berlin, then he led his section down to strafe a German airdrome. His guns hammered a parked Do–17 to pieces, then his own plane was riddled by the torrent of small-arms flak thrown at him from below. His windscreen was shattered and he was knocked unconscious by a slug that creased his head. He came out of it in a climb, with blood oozing down his face. Wiping away the blood he gazed at his instruments and was sickened when he saw the engine temperature gauge soar into the red. Another P–51 flew alongside and the pilot told Godfrey that he was streaming glycol. At first Godfrey panicked and got ready to bail out over Germany. But a squadron mate, Fred Glover, suggested an unorthodox way to keep his engine cool and Godfrey settled back in the cockpit and did as Glover suggested.

Godfrey started pumping the primer, which fed raw fuel into the cylinders and gave a cooling effect. The wobble pump was hard to work, but Godfrey kept at it and watched the needle swing back into the green. Escorted by the other P–51s, Godfrey kept pumping and kept flying. He had more than 650 miles to go.

When Godfrey's Mustang had first been hit, he blew the canopy, preparatory to bailing out. Now, as he worked the heavy primer back and forth, his body was lashed with a tornado of cold air blasting throughout the cockpit. Godfrey descended, seeking warmer air, and crossed the Dutch coast at 4,000 feet, a dangerous altitude. But no German fighters appeared. Constant friction against the pump handle wore a hole in his glove, then his hand; the pump and the remains of his flying glove became wet and slippery with blood. But Godfrey forgot the pain at the sight of England and he pumped on, numb with cold and enduring a splitting headache. The coast slipped underneath his wing and he put the Mustang down at the nearest field. Later, Godfrey calculated that he had pumped the primer more than 3,000 times, but it had saved him from captivity.

Despite his experience, the lure of parked German aircraft sitting like so many fat ducks on a pond was irresistible to Godfrey. On August 24, the 4th Group was providing escort for B–17s, but the Luftwaffe failed to react as the formation crossed the enemy coast. Godfrey was itching for action, for more kills to add to his score. With the Big Friends well protected by swarms of Mustangs, Godfrey led his section down to the deck to seek targets of opportunity. He located a German airdrome packed with Ju–52s. Remembering the last time he had gone down to strafe, Godfrey hesitated, then pushed the stick over "for just one pass."

The Mustang howled down out of the sky and Godfrey's guns raked the ugly transport planes. No flak rose to meet him, so he turned and came back again, his wingman right behind him. Now machine-gun fire laced the air and Godfrey felt his plane quiver with strikes. An 88-mm shell burst under-

91

True meaning of airpower came home to Germans when long-range American fighters roamed at will across the Third Reich killing everything that moved. Trains, tanks and fighter airfields were prime targets for P–38s, P–47s, and P–51s who left scenes of destruction such as these in their wake.

neath him. Disregarding the tracers that were flying all around him, Godfrey made pass after pass at the field, watching his own bullets chew into the Ju–52s. A rain of slugs swept his Mustang from engine to tail. The big Merlin engine coughed, the rev counter sagged, then the engine slammed to a halt. The silence was awesome. Godfrey sighed deeply and dropped the nose of the P–51 and glided down to crash land in an empty field. He staggered out of the burning fighter and ran for some nearby woods.

Godfrey, half dead from cold and fatigue, wandered around Germany for four days before a German farmer took him prisoner at the end of a heavy pitchfork. As Godfrey was led away to a POW camp there were two thoughts uppermost in his mind: *How soon can I escape? Will my last kills of the Ju–52s be verified?*

At peak strength, Eighth Fighter Command contained three wings made up of five groups, about 1,000 fighter planes in all. The top-scoring groups in the European Theater at the end of the war were the 4th, with 1,006½ enemy aircraft destroyed; the 56th Group, with 1,006 destroyed, and not far behind, the 355th Group with 860 to its credit. Rivalry was especially fierce between Blakeslee's 4th and Colonel Hub Zemke's 56th, known as the "Wolfpack." Zemke's galaxy of aces equaled those of the 4th, and included such great pilots as Francis Gabreski, John C. Meyer, David C. Schilling, Gerald Johnson, Walker "Bud" Mahurin, and Robert S. Johnson, whose impatience to wage personal war with the Luftwaffe matched that of Johnny Godfrey.

Bob Johnson was an Oklahoman whose passion for flying was ignited when he was twelve; a fifteen-minute hop in a Ford Trimotor convinced him that he belonged to the sky, and that the sky belonged to him. Fully grown, Johnson stood less than five-feet-eight, but that was tall enough to pass an Air Force physical when he was twenty-one. He struggled through the exhilarating agony of cadet life at Kelly AFB and Randolph AFB in Texas, and in the summer of 1942 was given his wings and his commission as second lieutenant and, most precious of all, orders to report to the 56th Fighter Group, then based in Connecticut, to learn to fly Thunderbolts.

Before the Group's operational training was completed, eighteen young pilots lost their lives in accidents of one kind or another; the P–47 was hot and heavy, unlike anything the pilots had flown in advanced training at Kelly.

Johnson observed that if the Group had been flying a fighter less sturdy than the Thunderbolt, even more men would have died.

One pilot lost power on takeoff and smashed into the hard water of Long Island Sound doing 150 mph. The big fighter cartwheeled over and over, sending spray a hundred feet into the air, coming to rest in shallow water. Pilots of the 56th rushed to the water's edge, waiting for the crash boat crew to come out and pull the dead aviator from the battered P–47. But the pilot crawled out unaided and waded to shore suffering only from bruises and a lump on the head. When the 56th arrived in England to begin its combat tour, the pilots justifiably had confidence that the Jug could take any punishment the Germans could hand out.

The Wolfpack engaged the Luftwaffe in strength for the first time on April 29, 1943. The Group reeled from the encounter like a fighter stumbling from the ring with black eyes and a bloody nose; two Thunderbolts were shot down and three returned to base badly riddled with shell and bullet holes fired by Me–109 and FW–190 marksmen. The Wolfpack pilots soberly went about learning their craft, and seven weeks after they took the shellacking from the Germans the 56th began to take its revenge.

On June 12, an FW–190 was shot down over Belgium, and on the day following Hub Zemke bagged two more and Bob Johnson got his first. Zemke first congratulated Johnson on his kill, then proceeded to give him a tongue-lashing for leaving the formation. Johnson did his best to comply with Zemke's firm command *never* to leave formation to go off glory hunting on his own, but his natural aggressiveness somehow led him astray several times thereafter, and he stayed in hot water with the Wolfpack's acid-tongued CO for a long time.

Shortly after his first victory, Bob Johnson underwent a nightmarish experience in his Thunderbolt that almost completely unnerved him. The 56th Group was escorting Big Friends on a strike deep inside France, and north of Rouen the sky seemed to explode with FW–190s dropping out of the sun. Johnson, obediently holding formation, was shocked as hammer-blows began beating at his airplane. *Blam! Blam! Blam!* Cannon shells smash against the armor plate at his back, rip through his wings, shatter the canopy. The Focke-Wulf riding his tail now opens up with machine guns, and Johnson feels his P–47 shake and shiver as the German pilot whipsaws his bullets through the cockpit. A slug creases his nose, starting the blood flowing; another tears the wristwatch from his arm; two more zip across his right leg, tearing the cloth of his flight suit and gouging flesh, but Johnson does not feel the pain. He sits frozen in the cockpit, awaiting death. Cannon shells and machine-gun slugs hammer at his fighter, the jarring impacts stabbing him back to action. He frantically unbuckles his seat belt and claws loose the leg straps. He has only one thought: *Get out!*

But before Johnson can do more, the P–47 is lashed again by a storm of exploding cannon shells and the fighter jerks out of control and starts spinning through the sky. Then, the final calamity: fire gushes into the cockpit. The out-of-control Jug whips downward, pluming smoke, spins through the formation of B–17s and miraculously misses all of them. Johnson, panic welling up uncontrollably, reaches up and grabs the bar just over his helmet

The Wolfpack. Left to right, standing: Francis Gabreski, Robert S. Johnson, Walker "Bud" Mahurin, Robert Landry. Seated on wing, Walter Cook and David Schilling. Pilots like these were as well known among the Luftwaffe as they were to their own commanders.

and jerks the canopy backward. The oval plexiglas dome moves only six inches, then jams. Johnson braces his boots against the instrument panel and heaves with strength born of desperation, but the canopy will not budge. He is trapped inside the burning fighter. Johnson is terrified at the thought of roasting alive, then being scattered over foreign soil when the Thunderbolt smashes itself against the earth.

Suddenly, the fire is gone.

Johnson reacts quickly, pulling back on the stick, and his heart leaps when the fighter responds; the Jug is coming out of its earthward plunge. It levels off. Cold air beats against Johnson's face through gaping holes in the canopy. He manages to get his head and shoulders through the shattered dome, but his parachute will not clear. He slumps back in the seat and wonders what to do next.

Thunderbolt pilot miraculously escaped death when he brought his crippled, flaming fighter back from strafing attack after German flak shot him down. Pilot crash-landed and crawled clear before fire gutted his plane.

He does not believe that the crippled fighter can be flown across the Channel. He swings to the south, determined to crash-land near the Spanish border and cross over, somehow making it back to England. He keeps a southerly heading for only a few minutes; the P–47 is still flying and the early panic is gone. Johnson swings the massive nose back to the west, toward England.

A new problem arises. The merciless cannonading his P–47 has received has shot away most of his flight instruments, severed his oxygen line, and, worst of all, holed the reservoir of hydraulic fluid, which is whipped into his eyes by the howling blast of air pouring through the canopy. The fluid almost blinds Johnson, and the pain is unbearable. He swabs at his face with a handkerchief, rubbing away the stinging, viscous fluid. His vision clears slightly and there, directly in front of him and only minutes away, is the English Channel. Something else slides into his field of vision: another airplane easing up alongside his own. Through narrow slits in a grotesquely puffy face Johnson squints hard at his company. New terror rises. Flying beside him is a brand-new, dappled blue Focke Wulf 190 with a gleaming yellow nose.

The German pilot slides closer. Only yards separate the two fighters; one, an oil-streaming, shot-up wreck, the other, an airplane dazzling in its beauty. Johnson locks eyes with the German pilot briefly, then the German lets his gaze travel the length of the riddled Thunderbolt. His curiosity satisfied, the German throws Johnson a salute and banks gracefully away to fasten his sights on the P–47. He takes his time, and Johnson hunches himself down, waiting.

Then it comes, the even hammering of the German's machine guns. The Thunderbolt shudders all over again as the lead slugs tear through the tail, the wings, the fuselage. Johnson prays that cannon fire will not follow—and it does not. He guesses that the German has already used it up on some other victim. The merciless fusillade beats against the helpless Thunderbolt for long seconds, then stops. The German pulls his sleek fighter alongside the P–47 to see what keeps it flying. The German is so sure of his kill that he makes no attempt to force Johnson onto another course; the Jug is still pointed toward England when Johnson crosses the coast and bores on across the Channel, only 4,000 feet above the whitecaps.

Again the German tosses Johnson a salute, and again he slides back on

For many American fighter pilots and bomber crews, these silhouettes were the last things they saw on earth. Top, an Me-109 boring in for the kill; bottom, an FW-109 seen dead astern.

the Jug's tail to continue the symphony of death. Johnson braces himself in front of the armor plate and feels the thumping as the 7.9-mm slugs strike home. The pounding continues until Johnson wonders which will run out first, his nerve, the German pilot's ammunition, or the invisible glue that is keeping the Thunderbolt together.

The firing stops; it is the ammunition fired so carefully and without effect that runs out. The German pulls up for the last time for a final salute of admiration, then banks away, leaving Johnson alone over the Channel. Thirty long minutes later Johnson is putting the Thunderbolt down on his home base at Manston. The hydraulic lines have long ago been drained of fluid, but Johnson skillfully lands the hurtling fighter without flaps or brakes. He climbs from the shattered cockpit and starts counting holes. The sturdy Thunderbolt has been gouged twenty-one times by exploding 20-mm cannon shells, and more than 100 machine-gun slugs have sieved the airplane from propeller to rudderpost. The battered Jug is towed away to be scrapped, and the meat wagon comes to take Johnson to the hospital for patching.

Johnson was back in combat not long afterwards to begin running up his victory string. On October 10, 1943, the Wolfpack rendezvoused with more than one hundred B–17s en route home after plastering Münster with 500- and 1,000-pound bombs. The sky was alive with diving German fighters machine-gunning, cannonading, and rocketing the Flying Fortresses, several of which were already spiraling earthward in dives of death. Bob Johnson, whose wingman had been forced to abort the mission, threw his P–47 at a trio of German fighters, standing the Jug on its nose to get at an Me–110 before the German fighter could blow a straggling B–17 apart with its rockets. Johnson's guns flamed the Me–110, then he turned into an attacking FW–190 and flamed that one, too. But another 190 had leaped on the P–47's uncovered tail and poured bullets into the rudder. Johnson felt the rudder controls go slack and knew that the cable was shot away. He pulled away from the fight and decided to bail out; he did not relish the thought of another agonizing trip home in a crippled fighter. He undid the straps and threw back the canopy. One leg was over the side, then he changed his mind and dropped back in the seat. He experimented with the rudder trim tabs and discovered that they provided a minimum of lateral control. He decided to stick with the Jug and ride her home. He did, elated at the knowledge that the last FW–190 he bagged made five and he had become an ace!

On New Year's Eve, Johnson bagged nine and ten, and on January 13, 1944, he shot down his thirteenth. The foul European weather of winter— rain, sleet, snow, and leaden overcast—put a comparative lull in operations through the beginning of March, and Johnson was able to add only two more kills to his log. Then, on March 6, he took part in one of the wildest melees ever fought over Germany.

Hundreds of B–17s fought their way through heavy flak and fighter opposition to clobber Berlin and were trying to fight their way back when the P–47s were jumped by superior numbers of German fighters. In the initial

Occasional pin-point bombing, such as this strike on the Kronprinz Wilhelm railroad bridge across the Rhine River, helped cripple German transportation.

shock, about fifty Thunderbolts clashed head-on with about 150 FW–190s and Me–109s. As the fighters clawed to get at one another in the crowded sky, the Jug pilots had to fleetingly observe that Big Friends were falling in awesome numbers; some in flames, some simply blowing apart in the air, others victims of ramming by overexcited German fighter pilots. Thousands of machine guns laced the sky over Berlin. Parts of airplanes tumbled lazily through the air. Parachutes blossomed. Men were dying.

Johnson dived on a pair of Me–109s that were hounding a crippled B–17 trailing smoke. The Germans scattered at Johnson's approach, but he fastened his sights on one of the 109s that made the fatal error of trying to outdive the Thunderbolt and Johnson's guns chopped him to pieces. Moments later Johnson shot down another Me–109, driving his score to seventeen—all fighters. Colonel Zemke knocked down three during the wild fight, and although the loss to the Wolfpack was only one pilot and plane, the B–17s were savagely mauled; sixty-eight of the big bombers were shot down that day, trailing silver wreckage all the way to the target and back.

Despite the sickening losses sustained by Eighth Bomber Command on such strikes at Schweinfurt and Regensburg and Berlin, not once was any bomber formation turned back until its load of destruction was toggled. The escorting Little Friends began to offer more protection once they were allowed to fly some distance away from the bomber stream, placing themselves high above and far in front of the B–17s and B–24s. In this way, the P–47s and P–51s could begin to break up the German fighter attacks earlier and the bombers suffered less.

The duel for the skies over Germany continued almost without letup until the spring of 1945. The Wolfpack continued to flay the German fighters, but they took their losses, too. Francis Gabreski, the tough-looking pilot from Oiltown, Pennsylvania, fell captive to the Germans on his 193rd combat sortie. He had thirty-one air-to-air kills to his credit when he went down and, like Godfrey before him, had his sights set on at least fifty.

Gabreski took his squadron down to strafe a German airfield near Coblenz. Leading, Gabreski barreled his Thunderbolt across the airfield with guns blazing. He was so low that the tops of the hangars were *above* his canopy roof. *Whump!* Gabreski felt the Jug shudder violently. He was flying much too low and his four-bladed prop slammed into a mound of earth at the end of the field. A hurricane of ground fire stormed all around him. Gabreski

Deadly Me–109s in a killer pack streak across Germany to reach formations of American bombers before tons of destruction can be unloaded on cities and factories.

knew that if he tried to climb out his chances of survival were practically nonexistent. He chopped back on the power and bellied in at 200 mph at the edge of a tree line. The big fighter slewed, scattering dust in its wake. Gabreski, tightly strapped in, rode the seven-ton metal bronco to a standstill, threw open the canopy and hit the ground running. He managed to elude capture for five days until an alert German farmer—the country seemed to be crawling with pitchfork vigilantes—took him in tow and delivered him to

Stricken Fortress, knocked out of control when late bomb release caused a 500–pounder to shear its left horizontal stabilizer, loses altitude sharply.

The Dogfighters

a. Francis "Gabby" Gabreski, Wolfpack ace with thirty-one kills, had his sights set on fifty before he was captured.

b. First Lieutenant Robert W. Deiz was one of the crack pilots of the 99th Fighter Squadron.

Luftwaffe MPs. At the sight of the rough-looking American ace, the Luftwaffe interrogator brightened and said, "Hello, Gabby! We've been waiting for you."

Flak got Hub Zemke a few days before Christmas, 1944, and he sat out the rest of the war at *Stalagluft* One as senior officer present—and with seventeen kills to his credit.

Bob Johnson somehow escaped both flak and fighters to run his score to twenty-eight air-to-air kills before he was rotated back to the States.

Back at the prison camp, Johnny Godfrey fretted away his long captivity. He burned to return to Debden, where he could climb back into a Mustang

The Dogfighters

c. Famed actor, Clark Gable (right), left Hollywood's glitter to volunteer for Officer Candidate School at the age of forty-two. He rose to the rank of major and became one of the top gunnery officers of the 8th Air Force.

d. Lieutenant Vernon Richards flew a P–51 escorting heavy bombers on a raid against Third Reich industrial targets. Ink markings on his hand were remainders of rendezvous points, radio frequency and compass bearing for route home.

and catch up with the other aces of Eighth Fighter Command who had been gunning down Germans while he wasted his time behind barbed wire. Twice Godfrey tried to escape, and twice he failed. Finally, on April 3, 1945, he succeeded in getting away. He walked south through wintry Germany, hoping to run into the advancing American troops. Once a friendly German farmer gave him shelter, hot food, and a bath. Godfrey kept slogging on, sometimes getting free rides aboard German trucks carrying guns to the Front. Instead of encountering American infantry, Godfrey blundered into a detachment of German Home Guards and was made prisoner again. He

105

The victor and the vanquished. Yankee bulldozer pushes aside crumpled remains of an Me–109 while a P–38 noses down for a landing.

learned what it was like to be strafed when the column was hammered mercilessly by low-flying P–47s.

Two weeks after his breakout, Godfrey was returned to another camp and once again found himself behind barbed wire. But the captivity was not to last long; the camp was soon overrun by U.S. troops, and Godfrey was turned loose to hitchhike back to Paris. He was soon back at Debden, but as it was apparent that the war was in its final days as far as Germany was concerned, no P–51 was forthcoming for Johnny Godfrey.

If he could not return to combat, there was at least one thing he could do: look at the 16-mm film taken from his wingman's gun cameras on the fateful day Godfrey was shot down. He hoped to prove that he had destroyed additional Ju–52s to run his score to thirty-eight. But when the grainy black and white film flickered on the screen Godfrey discovered quite another thing.

He watched the bullets spatter around one of the Ju–52s as his wingman fired. Then his pulse raced when he saw his own Mustang appear at the bottom of the screen. Reliving the mission, Godfrey was fascinated to see his own plane start climbing out after completing the low-level firing pass. Then Godfrey's jaw dropped. The film showed that his wingman kept firing as Godfrey climbed, the bullets slamming into Godfrey's own fighter.

The film was run through again, but there was no mistake: he had been shot down by his own wingman. Deflated, Godfrey walked out of the screening room and into the cold English spring.

Ground view of Me–262 reveals clean lines and underslung Junkers Jumo engines with nearly 2,000 pounds static thrust each. Nose housed four 30-mm cannons with 100 rounds per gun.

8/RACE FOR THE JETS

LATE IN 1944, as the Eighth Bomber Command's aerial assault against industrial targets in Germany reached crescendo, the crewmen of forty-eight B–17 Flying Fortresses en route to a target were given the greatest shock of their lives. The formation was bothered by only moderate flak and the American airmen hoped that the bombing and the return home would be logged as a milk run. Suddenly all thoughts of an easy mission vanished. Out of the sun dropped six propellerless twin-engined fighters moving faster than the Americans believed possible. They flashed through the B–17 formation with cannons flaming and were gone before the open-mouthed gunners could track them and return the fire.

The strange looking sharklike fighters made pass after pass at the Fortresses, and with each firing run some of the bombers lurched from the formation and spiraled earthwards or blew up in the sky. The German fighters shot down fourteen bombers within a few minutes, then whistled away untouched. The shaken pilots of the remaining B–17s closed ranks and flew on to bomb the target, sick with the knowledge that 140 of their wing mates were dead, wounded, or bound for captivity. And all it had cost the Germans was a few thousand pounds of cheap kerosene to fuel their new jet engines.

The entire Eighth Air Force was as disturbed as the B–17 survivors, who reported that the German jet fighters flew so fast that the gunners would have little chance at bringing their guns to bear in deflection shooting. Indeed, the jets were far swifter than even the newer-model P–51s, and American fighter commanders could no longer guarantee effective support for their Big Brothers.

Was it possible, the American air commanders asked, that at this late date the Luftwaffe could regain control of the air? If so, it meant that the combined U.S.–British bombing offensive would be brought to a halt until the

Allies could field an even superior jet fighter of their own. German industry could recuperate and continue to feed the war machine. Morale of the German people would soar. The war would drag on, conceivably ending with a 1918-type armistice instead of the unconditional surrender the Allies were committed to.

There was every reason to worry—but even the top air commanders could not know that Adolf Hitler, the "brilliant" tactician in war, had already made a decision concerning the jet fighters that sealed Germany's doom.

The idea of jet and rocket propulsion systems for aircraft was not new. In fact, on August 27, 1939, the world's first jet flight was successfully accomplished at the German Heinkel works when a Luftwaffe captain named Warsitz flew an experimental He–178 for six minutes at 2,000 feet. Ernst Heinkel was so excited that he called General Ernst Udet at four in the morning to break the great news. Two days later a second flight of the He–178 was staged for Udet and other ranking Luftwaffe officers, who still remained skeptical. After all, the war that was coming would be short, and there were plenty of Stukas and Me–109s to take care of the opposition.

A year later to the day, the Italians demonstrated that they, too, had jet capability by flying a Caproni-Campini turbine design. A few months afterward the British put their hat in the reaction ring by test-flying the first Gloster-Whittle jet. That same year, on October 1, the American Bell twin-jet XP–49 Airacomet whistled through California skies to become the first U.S. entry in the sweepstakes of the future.

Although the Germans began the war with an eighteen-month advantage in jet propulsion over its enemies, this priceless technological jump was not to be pressed to its fullest until it was too late. Political interference with what was purely a matter of military common sense and military need cost the Luftwaffe dearly. In 1942, it was clear that the Germans were not capable of bringing the British Empire crashing down with a rain of bombs on her large cities. It was equally clear that the Americans were gearing their bomber production to large, four-engined heavies capable of ranging across the Reich, using England as a permanently anchored aircraft carrier. It should have been obvious that Germany's future needs would be for as many high-performance interceptors as possible to counter the threat of destruction from the air. And, to many German builders and Luftwaffe generals, it *was* obvious; but Hitler, Goering, and other Nazi party members were using clouded crystal balls when the critical decisions were made.

The most promising design available to the Luftwaffe was the rakish Me–262, a single-seat twin-jet fighter powered with Junkers Jumo turbojet engines slung underneath the wings. The engines developed a total of just under 4,000 pounds of thrust, giving the airplane a maximum speed at altitude of 540 mph in level flight and a service ceiling of just under 40,000 feet. Designer Willy Messerschmitt had completed the first Me–262 airframe as early as November 1938, but the "Stormbird," as he called it, did not receive its engines until two years later. The fighter was first tested in flight in March 1941, and the pilot was enthusiastic. The Me–262 responded beautifully, accelerated wonderfully, and demonstrated excellent turn characteristics. Improvements were made, and the Stormbird proved capable of diving in excess of 625 mph, near the threshold of the speed of sound, and the fighter had a range of 650 miles, more than enough to allow it to reach any enemy bomber formation before vital targets could be threatened, long enough to allow it to stay in the air and do real damage.

Hitler allowed further work to be carried out on the Me–262, but to the consternation of the Luftwaffe fighter chiefs he could not make up his mind whether the new and sensational weapon should be employed as a fighter or as a bomber. General of the Fighter Arm Adolf Galland pleaded with his superior, Goering, to have the Me–262 put into large-scale production as a fighter so that the mounting British and American bombing raids could be brought to a halt, but all that came out of Hitler and the High Command was orders that amounted to wait-and-see. Months of time precious to the Germans was lost.

It wasn't until late in 1943 that Hitler decided that the Stormbird was worth developing, after all. This was at a time when the British were coming over almost every night with a thousand heavies, and the Americans were pulverizing German plants by day. This was at a time when 8th Fighter Command's Mustangs, Thunderbolts, and Lightnings were sweeping across Germany, proving their superiority to the older Me–109s. And yet, the question Hitler posed to Willy Messerschmitt through Goering was: *How many bombs can the Me–262 carry?* It was admitted that the plane could carry at least a pair of 500-pounders, perhaps more. But Hitler could not seem to grasp the hard facts that so weighted the Me–262 would sacrifice

The destructive power of the Me–262's heavy cannon is seen in these two photos. Left, the entire elevator of this B–17 was shot off. Somehow the bomber made it home. Below, this Fortress was nearly torn in two, but managed to stagger back to England.

its great speed advantage, that the plane could not be used as a dive-bomber, that high-level bombing was impractical because the plane could not be fitted with the proper bombsight, that operating jets at low altitudes is terribly wasteful of fuel, that, in other words, to use the Me–262 as a bomber would be the same as using a thoroughbred race horse to tow a beer wagon. Hitler could only think of two things: that the Me–262 would be able to stop the coming Allied invasion of France and that the Me–262 could be used to drop bombs on England. He told General Galland, "At last this is the blitz bomber!" Stunned, Galland listened as orders were given to start producing these Blitz bombers with all possible haste.

Willy Messerschmitt had other surprises in store for Allied fighter and bomber pilots. Since 1938, this energetic little designer had nourished a dream of producing the world's first rocket fighter. In April 1941, the dream came true with the first successful test flight of the Me–163, a fat, heavy little fighter only eighteen feet, eight inches long. Known as the Komet, the chubby interceptor was flown on May 10, with test pilot Heinz Dittmar at the controls, to maximum performance; the Komet reached a speed of 623.8 mph before its 3,750 pound thrust rocket engine cut out. Further trials showed that the Komet could literally rocket itself from ground level to 40,000 feet in less than three minutes. The great drawback of the Me–163, despite its sensational performance, was the fact that its five tons of fuel lasted only about five minutes, giving the airplane an operating radius of only about fifty miles. This was good enough, however, if the Komets were based near the main Allied strategic targets. Accordingly, the Me–163s were put into production at a rate of 100 per month and as soon as they were rolled from the production lines were formed into squadrons based deep inside Germany where they could offer protection to German factories and oil-processing facilities.

On August 5, 1944, American B–17s and P–51s ran afoul of the new German rocket fighters over Magdeburg. Three Me–163s streaked at the bomber formation from an altitude of 35,000 feet, their path in the sky traced by fire and vapor trails. The bomber crewmen braced themselves for the onslaught, but the German rocket pilots decided to attack the escorting P–51s instead. The Mustang pilots poured maximum boost to their engines, but the Komets were at least 100 mph faster and within seconds were

One reason why Eighth Bomber Command gave thanks that few of the German jets arrived too late. With wing blown off, hapless B–17 flops over on its back to begin death spiral.

fastened to the tails of the P–51s and firing. One, two, three the P–51s were shot out of the sky. Then the Komets' rocket motors sputtered to a stop and they glided away to land, proving that they could penetrate the fighter screen with ease. Many B–17s and B–24s fell to the lightning attacks delivered by the Me–163s; there simply was no way to stop them. However, many of the Komets were shot down by canny P–51 pilots who were able to get the jump on the rocket planes after the motors had stopped; the Germans then were piloting only heavy gliders against the deadliest prop-driven fighter in the world. The rocket fighter was never decisive in the air battle over Germany because there were too few of them and because the Eighth Air Force concentrated its bombs on the Messerschmitt factories and assembly points, destroying them before they ever left the ground.

Hitler's insistence upon turning the Me–262 into a bomber resulted in dozens of the sleek craft lumbering off to battle hung with a ton of bombs slung underneath their wings. They managed to bomb and strafe American positions during the Battle of the Bulge, but as it turned out not one of them reached England to bomb the invasion ships as they lay at anchor, nor did they devastate the beaches at Normandy, as Hitler hoped they would. The introduction, late in 1944, of the Arado 234B twin-jet bomber and reconnaissance craft allowed half of the production run of Me–262s to be diverted to the

Luftwaffe's fighter arm, and in October of that year, General Galland at last received permission from Goering to form an elite squadron of jets to do battle with the bombers. Galland chose one of his top-scoring aces, Major Walther Nowotny with 258 kills, to lead this first all-jet unit. Nowotny was killed on his own field in a landing accident shortly after the unit, JG 7, was formed, but the squadron went on to shoot down more than fifty Allied fighters and bombers within a few weeks' time.

Now Galland was called upon by Hitler to form an entire wing of Me–262s. Galland wished that the Fuehrer had given this order a year earlier, but in the waning weeks of the war he put together a second squadron, made up of the most experienced fighter pilots still alive in Germany. Almost all of them had been in combat since 1939, and most of them had been wounded more than once. The Squadron of Experts, as it was called, was based near Munich at a specially camouflaged airfield that pro- vided concrete revetments against incessant American air attacks. Galland fitted the Me–262s with newer weapons, including wing racks carrying two dozen 30-caliber rockets. In April 1945, only three weeks before the sur- render of Germany, Galland, a three-star general, led his Experts against American bombers.

Near Landsberg, Galland and his pilots whistled down on a formation of Martin B–26 Marauder medium bombers. Galland got within 600 yards of the formation and let fly with a salvo. The rockets spread, trailing white streamers of smoke, and crashed into the American mediums. One B–26 blew up immediately, and another spun dizzily out of the formation, part of

Another Luftwaffe surprise was Willy Messerschmitt's Me–163 Komet, an all-rocket interceptor. Me–163s went into combat late in 1944, but because they were tricky to handle, many exploded on the ground during landing.

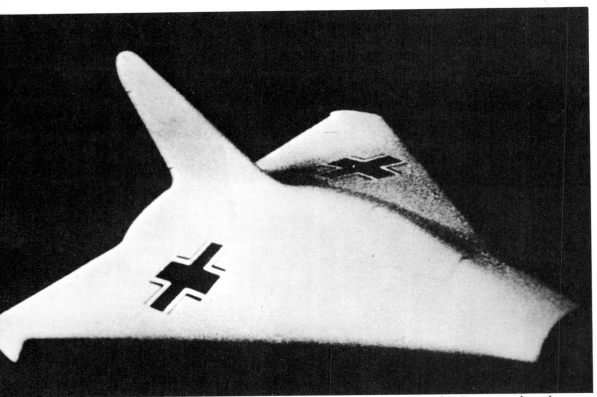

The revolutionary Jaeger P–13 was under development by the Germans when the war ended. This wind tunnel model of ram jet fighter indicated supersonic speeds of nearly 1,500 mph.

the tail and one wing missing. His armament gone, Galland banked away, excited at the knowledge that his jets could tear apart enemy bombers from a range that left the American gunners helpless.

The jubilation was far too late. Despite the superiority of the German jets, the Third Reich was overwhelmed by the thousands of American and British planes that ranged across Germany, bombing and strafing airfields and factories, crippling the jet program before it could become truly effective. More than half of the Me–262 production was destroyed on the ground by low-flying Mustangs, Thunderbolts, Lightnings, Typhoons, and Tempests.

Sleek British Meteor jet fighter was in production before the war ended, but none were committed to combat.

Galland flew his last jet mission on April 26, again against the B–26s. He shot down one Marauder, crippled another, and while turning away from the Americans an alert P–51 pilot got on his tail and riddled the Me–262 with 50-caliber slugs. Galland nursed the crippled jet back to his airfield and was forced to land through a web of Thunderbolts strafing the airdrome from every direction. Lieutenant General Galland, with 103 confirmed kills, jumped out of the world's greatest fighter plane and ended the war in a smoking bomb crater, watching helplessly as the P–47s shot his remaining jets to scrap metal.

117

Japanese air power dealt American forces a crushing blow at Pearl Harbor on December 7, 1941.

9/HELLCATS AND ZEROS

ONE OF THE GREAT SAGAS in the history of air warfare is the story of how the pilots of the U.S. Navy, Marines, and Army Air Forces fought their way to victory in the vast arena of the Pacific Ocean after being all but wiped out in the first disastrous days of the war with Japan. The road that led to the enemy mainland was long, rugged, and bloody.

It was a fighter pilot's war every painful step of the way.

It is Sunday morning, December 7, 1941. At Pearl Harbor, on Oahu in the Hawaiian chain of islands, many people are still asleep. Lying at anchor in the harbor are nine American battleships, six cruisers, and many other destroyers, seaplane tenders, and various kinds of supply ships. Except for three aircraft carriers that are at sea, almost all of the U.S. Navy's combat force is bottled up inside Pearl Harbor—a concentrated target inviting attack. But America is at peace, and nobody is expecting, or is prepared for, an attack. England has been fighting for survival against the Germans for more than a year, but America has remained firmly neutral, and hopes to remain so despite strong indications that Japan is planning war in order to wrest control of the Pacific away from America and the British Empire.

In the murky interior of a U.S. Army mobile radar station on Oahu sits Sergeant Joe Lockard, his eyes glassy from peering into the round glass radar tube for nearly four hours. He has watched the needle sweep monotonously around and around, picking up only ground echo and known landmarks. Suddenly, at 6:45 A.M., Lockard snaps alert; a new blip jumps to life on the screen. The needle sweeps around again, and the blip is still there, but moving closer. Lockard watches the progress of the blip, then picks up his telephone receiver and calls his immediate superior and reports that an

119

unidentified aircraft, possibly hostile, is bearing down on Oahu. Lockard is told to forget the sighting, that it probably means nothing, that the set is probably out of order. Lockard knows better; the set is new and works perfectly. He stays glued to the radar set. The blip stays on the screen. What Lockard has picked up is a Japanese Zero floatplane launched from a cruiser to scout Pearl Harbor and bring back information to the main Japanese battle fleet making its way to Hawaii. At 7:17 A.M., Lockard's set begins to blaze with blips, looking like swarming fireflies on a summer night. Astonished, and alarmed, Sergeant Lockard estimates that "many, many" aircraft are heading straight for Pearl Harbor, and are less than 150 miles away. Again Lockard calls in to his superior, who acts annoyed, telling the sergeant that some B–17s are due in about that time and obviously what Lockard sees on the tube are his own airplanes. Lockard doesn't believe this, but all he can do is watch the blips come closer.

Exactly thirty-eight minutes later, at 7:55 A.M., the first of 353 Japanese twin-engined bombers, dive bombers, and fighters appears over Pearl Harbor and the destruction begins. Bombs scream down from the clear blue sky, smashing into battleships, ripping up airfields, exploding inside barracks, tearing up warehouses, setting off ammunition dumps, and flaming huge aviation fuel storage tanks.

When the high-level bombers have done their work, and while the dive bombers are working over untouched targets, the fast Zero fighters drop down almost to the deck and begin vicious strafing runs. The Japanese pilots are stunned at the sight of American fighter planes lined up in immaculate rows, wingtip to wingtip, as though waiting for inspection. Dozens are shot to shreds on single firing passes. Army and Navy pilots, frantically struggling into flight gear while on the run, rush across Oahu's main airfields at Ford Island, Hickam and Wheeler Fields, shouting for the ground crews to get the fighters ready for combat ten times as fast as they have ever done before. Men are shot down by strafing Zeros before tanks can be fueled, guns loaded, or engines warmed. Incredibly, American fighter aircraft have been drained of fuel and stripped of ammunition and placed in inviting rows because the military authorities at Pearl Harbor feared sabotage by the island's Japanese more than they feared an attack from the sky.

A handful of American fighter pilots manages to get airborne to wade into the swarms of Japanese aircraft circling overhead. Among them were

A formidable opponent was the Mitsubishi Zero fighter. Agile, quick-climbing and fast, the Zero commanded respect from American fighter pilots, some of whom had the chance to fly captured models.

two young Army lieutenants, George Welch and Kenneth Taylor. Flying Curtiss P–40B Tomahawks, the two pilots engaged a dozen Japanese dive-bombers attacking the Marine air base at Ewa. Both Taylor and Welch shot down three of the enemy bombers apiece, then landed to rearm. Welch got off all right, but Taylor was shot down by a low flying Japanese attacker, who was shot down in turn by Welch.

When the last attacking Japanese plane droned away to the west, the stunned survivors at Pearl Harbor counted the damage. Five battleships—*Arizona, California, Oklahoma, Nevada,* and *West Virginia*—were either sunk or rendered useless, and thirteen other ships lay holed and smoking. More than 150 Navy fighters had been destroyed, and the Army Air Force sustained a loss of 151 fighters and bombers, almost all of them on the ground. The dead amounted to 2,844, and another 1,178 were wounded. The attack on Pearl Harbor was the worst defeat for American arms in history, but it cost the Japanese only twenty-nine airplanes and fifty-five pilots and crewmen. Had American fighter planes been ready and waiting, as warnings indicated they should have been, Pearl Harbor would probably have been a Japanese defeat instead.

The Japanese were victorious everywhere in the Pacific. Wake Island fell, and the Philippines, then the British were forced to surrender Singapore. The endless stretch of ocean was now virtually a Japanese lake. But even in the smoke of defeat, American planners were planning the long march to Tokyo. The strategy was as simple as it was demanding: to seize one Japanese-held island after another, using them as steppingstones, creating forward air bases with which to someday smash at the homeland of the enemy with giant bombers—bombers that were still on the drawing boards. Before this could come to pass the Americans would have to fight with what they had. Above all, the few precious carriers in the Pacific—the *Enterprise, Lexington,* and *Saratoga*—would have to protected by their own shipboard fighting planes, allowing the carrier-based dive and torpedo bombers to seek out and destroy Japanese ships.

On February 20, 1942, the carrier *Lexington* was sent on a mission deep into the South Pacific, toward Rabaul, where enemy convoys frequently passed. Aboard the *Lexington* was Air Group Six, flying chunky, square-winged Grumman F4F–4 Wildcats, a powerful fighter carrying six .50-caliber guns and powered by a 1,200-hp Twin Wasp engine that gave the folding-wing fighter a speed of 320 mph at 18,000 feet. Fitting the Wildcat with a pair of external fuel tanks, thus raising the total to 260 gallons, gave the fighter a range of just over 1,000 miles at slow cruising speed. The F4F Wildcat could never be called handsome, even by its designers, but it was long-legged and rugged, and that is what counted most with the men who flew her.

While the *Lexington* steamed toward Rabaul, a constant fighter screen

The mainstay of Navy and Marine pilots in the early Pacific War was the chunky Grumman F4F Wildcat.

American pilots dueled often with Japanese bombers called "Betty."

circled overhead. These Combat Air Patrols stayed aloft until fuel ran low, then were replaced by a fresh CAP catapulted from the carrier deck. While still many hours away from Rabaul, the *Lexington* was discovered by a multiengine Japanese reconaissance plane that quickly got off the carrier's position before being shot down by one of the CAP pilots, Lieutenant Commander John S. Thach. Not long afterwards a dozen Japanese twin-engine bombers known as "Bettys" were streaking for the *Lexington*. The Betty was fast and heavily armed, carrying both machine guns and 20-mm cannon in the nose and tail. Commander Thach and his five pilots managed to shoot down six of the bombers and were busily engaged with the survivors when yet another wave of nine Bettys was spotted on the *Lexington's* radar. Six more Wildcats were scrambled from the carrier deck to head off this new threat.

Leading the pack was Lieutenant Edward "Butch" O'Hare, a stocky aggressive fighter pilot who was destined to make history in the following frantic minutes. O'Hare and his wingman were first to see the oncoming wave of bombers, flying in a flawless V formation only fifteen miles from the vulnerable carrier. O'Hare's flight had scattered after leaving the carrier in order to cover a wider sweep area, so O'Hare and the other F4F dived into the enemy bomber stream by themselves. O'Hare's wingman discovered that his guns were jammed, so he broke off the engagement, and Butch O'Hare was left to face the nine Bettys alone.

O'Hare waded into the rear of the Japanese formation, his guns blazing.

123

Fatigue overcomes the unsung heroes of the Pacific war, the hardworking "Airedales," carrier deck crewmen who launched the fighter planes and their pilots on strikes against the enemy.

Two of the bombers started smoking, then the American pilot watched as engines on both planes tore from their mountings, causing the bombers to tumble wildly into the sea from 10,000 feet. O'Hare shifted the nose of his blue-winged fighter until the sights were lined up on a third bomber, then he pressed the firing button again. The heavy .50-caliber slugs ripped into the Betty and it staggered in the air, lost its left engine and flopped down, leaving a greasy black trail of smoke in the sky. O'Hare bored into the center of the Japanese formation, his stocky Wildcat caught in a web of tracers fired by the Japanese gunners.

While O'Hare was dueling against overwhelming odds, Thach and the others had shot down or crippled all nine of the first wave of Bettys and were climbing hard to help O'Hare. Thach watched in admiration as O'Hare made his firing passes "exactly the way that we had practiced. I could see three blazing Japanese planes falling between the formation and the water—he shot them down so quickly."

O'Hare paid no attention to the deadly streams of fire being poured at him. He carefully closed the range on a fourth Betty and pressed the button. His guns chattered briefly and the bomber lurched from the formation and spiraled down to the sea. By this time the remainder of the enemy force was at that point in space where the bombs could be released. O'Hare, knowing that the safety of more than a thousand men on the *Lexington* was in his hands, flung his fighter head-on against the bombers and clamped down on the trigger. A fifth Betty flamed up and spun out. O'Hare sprayed the others with bullets until, one by one, his guns fell silent.

Four minutes, five planes shot down: it was incredible shooting, and O'Hare's heroism earned him the Congressional Medal of Honor.

By the time O'Hare ran out of ammunition, Thach and the other F4Fs reached the four surviving Bettys, shot down two of them and sent the other two back across the ocean with smoking engines and dead crewmen aboard. The *Lexington* was saved for the long war that lay ahead.

This early clash in the air between carrier pilots and Japanese bombers proved that the only effective defense of ships, whether carrier or otherwise, lay in the hands of skilled and aggressive fighter pilots.

Throughout the early part of 1942, American carriers launched their

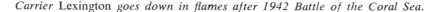

Carrier Lexington *goes down in flames after 1942 Battle of the Coral Sea.*

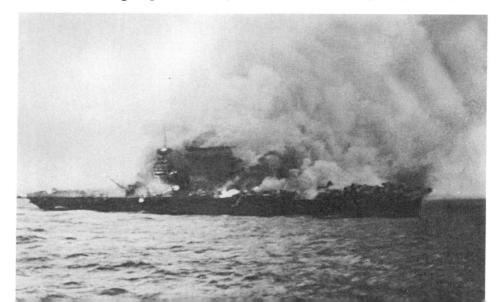

planes against targets in the Marshall and Gilbert Islands, small atolls with such names as Kwajalein, Roi, Makin, and Wotje. These raids were little more than pin-pricks, but they alarmed the Japanese and made Americans feel that they were on the offensive. On March 4, Task Force 16, commanded by tough Vice-Admiral William F. "Bull" Halsey, struck at Marcus Island, only a thousand miles from the Japanese homeland. On April 18, General James Doolittle led sixteen Army Air Force B–25 bombers off the carrier *Hornet* to lay bombs on Tokyo. Late that same month, a Japanese striking force set out to occupy Port Moresby in New Guinea, almost at Australia's doorstep. Bull Halsey ordered the carriers *Yorktown* and *Lexington* to spearhead a small interception force to engage the Japanese in the Coral Sea, to stop them there before Australia could be threatened.

The battle opened on May 7 with American and Japanese planes clashing in the air and smashing at each other's ships. The Japanese carrier *Shoho* was sent to the bottom less than forty minutes after she was sighted. Wildcat pilots shot down nine of twenty-seven Japanese bombers shortly before dark, and eleven others were blasted out of the sky by antiaircraft gunners who watched in amazement as some of the enemy bomber pilots, confused and low on fuel, tried to land on the American carriers. The battle resumed the following morning. *Yorktown* took torpedo hits and shuddered when two heavy bombs crashed through her flight deck. *Yorktown* dodged a swarm of torpedoes only to be hit by a bomb that set fires raging below decks. The enemy carrier *Shokaku* was dive-bombed and limped away from the battle. When

Launch! Grumman F6F Hellcat roars from flight deck to intercept Japanese strike force.

Douglas SBD Dauntless dive bombers nosing down to attack Japanese shipping. Fighter planes usually flew top cover.

the fighting ended early in the afternoon *Yorktown's* fires were under control, but the *Lexington,* on fire and listing badly, had to be abandoned. The Navy had lost thirty-three planes, the Japanese, forty-three. Although the losses were about equal, the Battle of the Coral Sea was nevertheless an American victory; the Japanese thrust toward Port Moresby was stopped.

The Japanese then moved toward strategic Midway Island, next to Hawaii the most valuable American outpost in the Pacific. If the Japanese managed to take Midway, only 1,200 miles northwest of Hawaii, not only Pearl Harbor, but the American mainland would be endangered. It was at Midway that the Mitsubishi Zero fighter temporarily gained air superiority over the best interceptors the Marine Corps could throw at them.

The Zero was the finest Japanese fighter to see active combat in any numbers during World War II; more than 10,000 were built between 1941 and 1945. The Zero was lightweight, curved, and graceful looking. The wings were only thirty-six feet long, the plane weighed only 6,000 pounds loaded, and, powered by a 1,120-hp radial engine, the agile little fighter could fly at nearly 350 mph. Zeros carried both machine guns and 20-mm cannon, they could climb like the wind and could outturn anything the Americans could send out against them. To achieve this hornetlike agility the Zero sacrificed armor plating for the pilot and the heavier self-sealing fuel tanks and, in some cases, even the radios were removed to further lighten the plane. Those shore-based Navy, Marine Corps, and Air Force pilots who met the Zero for the first time when the battle for Midway opened quickly learned just how great a fighter the Zero was.

127

Steaming for Midway on June 4, 1942, were four Japanese carriers—the ones that had struck at Pearl Harbor—two battleships, three cruisers, and a dozen destroyers. A Navy PBY flying boat discovered this massive armada moving on Midway on the early hours of the 4th, and the battle began. The Air Force and the Navy sent out a mixed force of thirty-eight bombers to strike at the Japanese, but the Zeros cut them to ribbons. Only half of them returned; the others had been shot down into the sea. Well-trained Marine fighter pilots tried to dogfight with the Zeros in the Marines' slow, clumsy F2A Brewster Buffalos. Twenty-four Buffalos went out, only ten returned. Fifteen TBD Devastators of Torpedo Squadron Eight went after the Japanese ships at low level, and every one was shot down. Finally, a squadron of SBD Dauntless dive bombers reached the Japanese fleet at a time when three of the carriers were loaded with Zeros and bombers taking on fresh fuel and ammunition. The SBDs plunged down in perfect dives and, one after the other, the Japanese carriers were torn apart by 1,000-pound bombs. They went under, carrying with them the elite of Japan's fighter pilots and their planes. Later in the battle the remaining enemy carrier was sent to the bottom. With his air power gone, Admiral Chuichi Nagumo had no choice but to retreat with his battleships and his fully loaded troop transports. Midway was saved.

Losses on both sides were heavy. Besides the four carriers, the Japanese lost a cruiser, 234 planes, and 2,500 men. The Americans mourned the loss of the *Yorktown*, a destroyer, and 300 dead. Zeros and flak accounted for

Nakajima Jill braves tornado of steel to attack American carrier. Such suicide missions were costly to both sides.

132 U.S. planes shot down. Despite the tragic toll, Midway was the turning point in the Pacific war that was only six months old. After Midway, the Americans could begin the long march westward.

On August 7, 1942, the U.S. Marines stormed ashore at Guadalcanal Island in the first ground offensive operation against the Japanese. Guadalcanal was a hell of mud, sniper-infested palm groves, and swarming clouds of vicious mosquitoes whose malarial stings put out of action nearly as many men as did enemy bullets. The big island's only airstrip, Henderson Field, was taken by the 1st Marine Division, quickly repaired by Navy construction battalion workers, and received the fighters necessary to the defense of the island. During the bitter six-month struggle for Guadalcanal, all kinds of fighter planes, Marine, Navy, and Air Force alike, flew from Henderson and other airfields in the Solomon Islands group. It was a time of trial, of revealing shortcomings in American equipment, and, finally, a time of triumph.

The Army pilots had the worst time of all. The 18th Pursuit Group had been hurriedly equipped with Bell P–39D Airacobra fighters, sleek-looking, fast down low, and armed with a powerful 37-mm cannon firing through the nose, but hopeless when pitted against Zeros. The P–39 could not climb as fast as the Zero, certainly could not turn with the Zero, nor could it reach the Zero's high altitudes. An export version of this plane, known as the P–400, had been found so deficient by the British that it was refused; thus the U.S. 67th Fighter Squadron found itself saddled with P–400s at a time when Japanese fury was at its height. The P–400s were not even equipped with oxygen, which is mandatory when flying above 10,000 feet for any period of time, and pilots came off of patrols three miles in the sky seeing spots in front of their eyes and choking for breath. P–39 and P–400 pilots who engaged Zeros in dogfights were simply shot out of the sky. Later, P–39s were assigned to ground-support missions shooting up enemy shipping, gunning tanks, and strafing airfields, and the P–39 performed admirably at these tasks; they had the guns for it, and with a top speed of nearly 370 mph could outrun any pursuers when near the ground.

Army Air Force pilots who flew Curtiss P–40E Warhawks were much more fortunate, especially since they had the benefit of the experience of the "Flying Tigers," American volunteer pilots who flew for the Chinese Air Force against the Japanese starting shortly after the bombing of Pearl Harbor.

129

Japanese Betty, victim of F6F machine-gunning, heads for the sea wrapped in flames.

The Tigers had learned never to dogfight a Zero with a P–40, but instead to get an altitude advantage and then dive into enemy formations with all six .50-caliber guns blazing before breaking off combat.

Infantrymen have always envied fighter pilots for their comforts while not actually engaged in combat. Aviators usually sleep in clean beds, eat hot meals, and bathe as often as they like. But at Guadalcanal the pilots were little better off then the Marines slogging their way through the steaming jungles. The Japanese plastered the airfield almost every night with gunfire from heavy cruisers lying offshore and with bombs from overhead. Pilots and crewmen endured these earth-shaking bombardments from muddy shelters carved into the ground, emerging sleepless to face another cold K-ration breakfast. Fresh water was in short supply, and only the minimum was used for shaving out of steel helmets. Primitive laundries could not keep up with the demand, and soon the pilots' clothes began to rot in Guadalcanal's hot and soggy climate, and almost all of them developed maddening rashes. Despite the oppressive environment, the fatigue and skimpy rations, the fighter pilots of Guadalcanal demonstrated to the Japanese that they were deadly opponents.

Late on the morning of August 30, the F4F Wildcats of Marine Fighter Squadron 223 scrambled from Henderson Field to intercept a gaggle of Japanese Zeros and Betty bombers. The husky fighters got away, followed by a handful of Army P–40s. The Marines were led by Major John L. Smith, who had bagged fived Japanese planes in ten days. Smith got his Wildcats on top of the Japanese formation and attacked. In the wild melee that followed Smith shot down four Zeros and his teammates blew apart ten more. Four of the P–40s fell victim to the agile Zeros, but the overwhelming victory of the

130

Wildcats gave American morale a tremendous boost and proved that the Zero was by no means invincible. Fighting Squadron 223 was relieved in October, but not before accounting for 110 enemy planes. Smith was awarded the Medal of Honor for his aggressiveness and daring in hurling his outnumbered pilots against the Japanese day after day.

The tempo of battle increased as the Japanese managed to run ashore thousands of fresh infantrymen from destroyers and transports, and the Marines struggled to survive. Without air power, they would have been doomed. On November 7, a fleet of Japanese ships was seen approaching the western end of Guadalcanal and SBD Dauntless dive bombers and bomb-carrying F4F Wildcats of Marine Fighter Squadron 121 took off to smash them before they could put reinforcements ashore.

Leading the Marine Wildcats was Captain Joseph J. Foss, a tough, cigar-chomping South Dakotan who sported a brushy black mustache. Foss got his fighters to 15,000 feet, but before they could spot the enemy destroyers Foss managed to jump a flock of Zero floatplanes cruising serenely beneath the F4Fs. Foss shot down two of the Zeros, but his own plane was shot up by a determined Japanese gunner firing from less than fifty feet away. Foss recalled that "the line of bullets stitched right up the cowling and I pulled my head back because I thought I was going to get it in the teeth."

Alert deck officer pulled F6F pilot to safety after fiery landing aboard carrier Enterprise.

Whispering Death. Chance Vought F4U–1 Corsairs were feared by the Japanese pilots more than any other American fighter.

Foss's radio was shot out and he was unable to contact his squadron. Foss nursed his crippled airplane back to Henderson Field, but the engine sputtered and backfired, and when Foss was forced to fly into a rainstorm, he lost precious altitude and then he knew he would never make it back to Guadalcanal. The engine quit cold and Foss glided down to ditch about a mile from the beach fringing a moss-green island, hoping that the place was not crawling with Japanese. The Wildcat hit hard, the unlocked canopy slammed shut and Foss went down with the sinking fighter. He managed to open the canopy, propel himself out of the cockpit, and claw his way to the surface, where he spewed out salt water. Disentangling himself from the wet silk parachute, Foss inflated his Mae West and tried to paddle for the island, but the tide carried him back out to sea. It started raining, then it got dark. Cold, his skin shriveled from hours in the sea, Foss stayed afloat but he could not make it to shore. Then a light appeared, revealing to Foss a large native outrigger canoe. Were there Japs aboard? Foss had no way of knowing. He tried to paddle away.

Then he stopped. A voice called out in English. Foss excitedly shouted out, "Friend! American! Birdman! Aviator!" The canoe swung by the water-logged Marine and strong hands pulled him aboard. His rescuers were led by a missionary priest named Father de Stuyvesant. Foss was back in combat the next day, and went on to run his total air-to-air kills to twenty-six, the first American to top Eddie Rickenbacker's record set in 1918.

The most incredible shooting by any Marine in the Solomon Islands campaign was done by First Lieutenant James E. Swett, twenty-two, a Califor-

A quartet of Hellcats on the prowl.

nian who flew Wildcats with Fighting Squadron 221. It was on April 7, 1943, that Swett chiseled a name for himself on the stone of Marine Corps history.

The Japanese had finally been driven from Guadalcanal in February, but they still held the island fortress of Rabaul, 600 miles to the north. On April 7, Admiral Isoroko Yamamoto mustered more than 300 fighters and bombers and hurled them at Guadalcanal, determined to wipe out the Americans there. As the great enemy armada swept down the Solomons, Jim Swett was among the fighter pilots who rose to challenge.

Swett, who had never fired his guns in anger, waded into a skyful of Aichi 99 "Val" dive bombers, single-engine planes carrying a pilot and a rear gunner. Although Swett is excited at being in combat for the first time, he coolly lines up one of the Vals in his gunsight and bores in until only a hundred yards separate his Wildcat and the Val. He presses the firing button, his fighter vibrates with the rattle of the six .50 calibers and the Val lurches and spins away trailing flame. Swett eases stick and rudder over, lines up a second enemy dive bomber and fires a short burst. The Val explodes in a sheet of orange flame and oily black smoke. Swett follows a third Val down almost to treetop level over Florida Island, hits the trigger and sees the mottled brown monoplane come apart in the air. He hauls back on the stick and climbs for altitude.

The sky over the harbor is filled with Wildcats, Vals, Bettys, P–40s, and the newer twin-tailed P–38 Lightnings. Swett knows that Zeros are up there flying top cover for the Japanese bombers, but he disregards the threat and firewalls the throttle to hurl his F4F into a seven-ship formation of Vals that

133

are streaking down to unload their bombs on American shipping. Swett guns down his fourth, fifth and sixth Val, flying through the debris to get at number seven. Now low on ammo, Swett closes the range to within fifty feet; he is so close he can make out the features of the enemy gunner firing tracers from the rear cockpit. Swett feels the steadying chugging of his own guns, then watches as his seventh victim slides out of the sky.

He wheels his Wildcat through space and jumps on the tail of another Val. But this time the Japanese gunner facing him is a crack shot; bullets thud into the F4F and part of the canopy is shot away. Swett manages to kill the gunner with the final rounds from his fifties, then he pulls away and heads for home. Elation at having made seven kills in almost as many minutes is replaced by a sinking feeling when the engine, riddled with slugs, coughs into silence. Swett guides the heavy fighter to a rough ditching in the channel that separates Guadalcanal from Florida Island. Bruised and battered, Swett bobs up and down in his raft until a motor launch retrieves him from the water.

Swett's incredible performance was but one of many that day. The all-out Japanese aerial offensive failed because determined fighter pilots like Swett blew nearly forty Japanese aircraft out of the sky, while losing only seven planes of their own. In the face of such losses, the Japanese were forced to abandon mass air attacks in the Solomons. What Fighter Command had done to Goering's offensive in the Battle of Britain had been repeated half a world away.

At home, American industry forged new weapons for the men fighting their way westward across the Pacific. The fighter pilots needed planes to surpass the Zero, and they got them. From Chance-Vought came the F4U Corsair, a gull-winged fighter with a 2,250-hp radial engine. The Corsair earned from the Japanese the name "Whispering Death," and with good reason. The F4U could reach 40,000 feet and could fly at 425 mph. Japanese pilots feared the Corsair more than any other fighter; a postwar tally showed that F4Us shot down 2,140 Japanese aircraft while losing only 189 of their own. The Corsair's normal armament of six .50-caliber guns could be augmented with rockets, napalm canisters, and bombs. One mission in the Pacific saw an F4U loaded with two tons of bombs that were dropped in the Marshall Islands.

Replacing the F4F Wildcat was the Grunmman F6F Hellcat, which resembled the Wildcat only superficially. The new fighter flew at 376 mph, but more important than sheer speed was the Hellcat's improved rate of climb and its ability to turn with Zeros in a dogfight. The Hellcat had electrically operated flaps and gun-charging mechanisms, and could carry twice the ammunition load of the Wildcat.

This outstanding airplane proved itself again and again in the bloody air battles over the Pacific, but it was in 1944 that the F6F, flown by skilled pilots, came into its own. Two examples will drive home the point.

On June 11, 1944, the Americans struck at the Marianas island complex, made up of Saipan, Tinian, Rota, and Guam. From Saipan, the mighty B–29 Superfortresses of the 20th Air Force could begin the bombing of Japan itself, only 1,200 miles away. Preinvasion strikes by F6Fs, Corsairs, and Dauntlesses helped pave the way for the Marines of the 2nd and 4th Divisions storming ashore against determined Japanese resistance, and after bloody fighting the Marines gained a beachhead and started to push inland on Saipan. The Japanese sent a large task force to wipe out the American navel power supporting the Marines, and on June 19 the greatest aerial battle of the Pacific War to date was fought.

Four times the Japanese sent waves of every kind of fighter and bomber at the American fleet, and four times the Hellcat pilots drove them away. Earphones crackled with cries of "Tallyho!" and *"Banzai!"* The sky filled with white tendrils of tracers, blossoming black bursts of flak, and balls of orange flame as aircraft were flamed. The Japanese fought bravely as they always did, but these pilots were not the veterans of the early days, nor were they flying a superior fighter. They were slaughtered. When the battle died down at dusk and the remnants of the once-awesome enemy force limped away, they left at the bottom of the Pacific the blackened hulks of 336 destroyed Zeros, Jills, Bettys, Vals—everything they could throw at the Americans. Only twenty-six American planes had been lost to enemy action. For those who were there, the battle will always be remembered as "The Great Marianas Turkey Shoot."

On October 20, 1944, General Douglas MacArthur made good his promise of 1941, "I shall return," when he led an invasion force ashore in the Philippines. The U.S. Army was supported by a monstrous naval armada, Task Force 38, commanded by feisty little Admiral Marc A. Mitscher. Backing the Philippine invasion were sixteen carriers, six battleships, fifteen cruisers, and more than fifty destroyers. Among the carriers was the veteran *Essex,* home

Commander David McCampbell, Navy's top ace, in Hellcat cockpit.

to Air Group 15, commanded by Commander David McCampbell, who had graduated from Annapolis eight years before the war began. Four days after the invasion started, McCampbell made naval aviation history.

On October 24, the Japanese sent the greater part of their fleet against the Americans in the Philippines. Waves of fighters and bombers swept down on the vulnerable U.S. carriers. McCampbell's F6F is launched from *Essex*

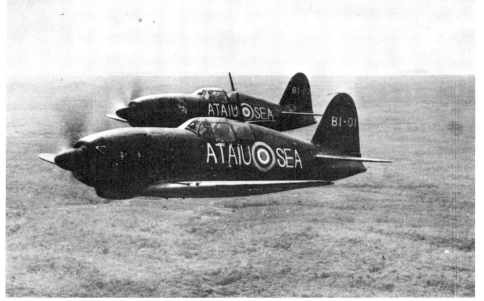

Latecomer to the war was the Japanese Mitsubishi Jack, a powerful interceptor which American pilots were glad weren't mass produced.

and his pilots reach one Japanese attacking force only twenty miles distant from the vulnerable carrier. Twenty bombers were protected by at least forty fighters stacked 3,000 feet above them. McCampbell split his flight of six Hellcats, sending four of the F6Fs to attack the bombers while he and his wingman, Lieutenant Roy Rushing, got above the Zeros. The odds were 20–1 against the Americans, but McCampbell knew that the American carriers would be in desperate shape if the Japanese force was not broken up.

Tallyho!

McCampbell and Rushing plunged downwards in a firing pass at the Zeros that were deployed in flawless V formations. The Hellcats' guns chattered briefly and two of the enemy fighters started burning and spun out of the sky. McCampbell shifted the nose of his F6F, lined up another unsuspecting Zero in his orange gunsight reticle, pressed the firing button, and watched pieces fly from the other plane before it exploded in flames. The Japanese finally awoke to the fact that they were under attack, but instead of breaking off to engage the lonely two F6Fs, they went into a Lufbery circle, each Zero flying on the tail of the plane ahead. Then, after the two Americans had made an unsuccessful firing pass at them, the Japanese broke their circle and

137

turned for land, strung out in a loose line-astern formation. McCampbell guessed, correctly, that the Japanese had been out so long looking for the American fleet that they were low on fuel and could not afford a dogfight. McCampbell and his wingman bored on after the retreating Japanese.

In the next sixty minutes, McCampbell's guns blasted seven more Japanese fighters out of the sky, making his total nine for the morning. McCampbell, escorted by Rushing, barely made it back to a safe landing on a strange carrier deck; only fumes were left in his tanks when the Hellcat rolled to a stop aboard *Langley*. Before the war ended, McCampbell ran his score to thirty-four, more than any other pilot wearing Navy wings. In commenting on his performance, McCampbell said modestly, "All you have to do is see 'em first. I am fortunate in having a wingman with eyes like an eagle. What I miss, he gets."

It was in the Pacific that America produced its greatest fighter pilot ace, Major Richard I. Bong, a twenty-four-year-old Fifth Air Force pilot who shot forty Japanese airplanes out of the sky at the controls of a Lockheed P–38. Bong was withdrawn from combat after gunning twenty-eight planes, but a few months later he wangled his way back to the Pacific as a gunnery instructor. He believed that the best way to instruct newer pilots was by showing them how it was done. This he proceeded to do, shooting down an additional twelve Japanese aircraft.

The war against Japan was carried right to the enemy's heartland. Before it ended on August 15, 1945, fighter pilots in P–51s, P–38s, F6Fs and Corsairs were roaming the length of Honshu, strafing and bombing at will from one end of the island empire to the other. For those who survived the early days, when just staying alive seemed to be some kind of miracle, it was sweet revenge.

End of the trail. An abandoned Zero, victim of strafing, sits rotting on Buna Strip in New Guinea.

TWELVE TOP FIGHTERS OF WORLD WAR II

The ranges listed for each fighter are maximum. Normal range, without external fuel tanks, was generally somewhat more than half of maximum.

UNITED STATES

GRUMMAN F6F–3 HELLCAT
Engine: 2000-hp Pratt and Whitney radial
Span: 42', 10"
Length: 33', 7"
Gross weight: 11,381 lbs.
Top speed: 376 mph
Range: 1590 miles
Armament: Six .50-caliber machine guns

LOCKHEED P–38G LIGHTNING
Engine: Two 1325-hp Allison
Span: 52'
Length: 37', 10"
Gross weight: 19,800 lbs.
Top speed: 400 mph
Range: 1670 miles
Armament: One 20-mm cannon, four .50-caliber machine guns

NORTH AMERICAN P–51D MUSTANG
Engine: 1695-hp Packard Merlin
Span: 37'
Length: 32', 3"
Gross weight: 10,100 lbs.
Top speed: 437 mph
Range: 2080 miles
Armament: Six .50-caliber machine guns

REPUBLIC P–47D THUNDERBOLT
Engine: 2300-hp Pratt and Whitney radial
Span: 40', 9"
Length: 36', 1"
Gross weight: 14,000 lbs.
Top speed: 426 mph
Range: 1800 miles
Armament: Eight .50-caliber machine guns

VOUGHT F4U–1 CORSAIR
Engine: 2250-hp Pratt and Whitney radial
Span: 40', 11"
Length: 33', 4"
Gross weight: 12,039 lbs.
Top speed: 425 mph
Range: 1562 miles
Armament: Six .50-caliber machine guns

GREAT BRITAIN

DE HAVILLAND MOSQUITO
Engine: Two 1620-hp Rolls-Royce Merlin
Span: 54', 2"
Length: 41', 2"
Gross weight: 20,600 lbs.
Range: 1770 miles
Top speed: 425 mph
Armament: Four 20-mm cannon

HAWKER HURRICANE IIB
Engine: 1280-hp Rolls-Royce Merlin
Span: 40'
Length: 32', 3"
Gross weight: 8470 lbs.
Range: 985 miles
Top speed: 340 mph
Armament: Eight .303-caliber machine guns

SUPERMARINE SPITFIRE XIV E
Engine: 2050-hp Rolls-Royce Griffon
Span: 36', 10"
Length: 32', 8"
Gross weight: 8500 lbs.
Top speed: 448 mph
Range: 850 miles
Armament: Two 20-mm cannon, two .50-
caliber machine guns

GERMANY

FOCKE-WULF 190F–3
Engine: 1700-hp BMW radial
Span: 34', 5"
Length: 29'
Gross weight: 10,850 lbs.
Top speed: 394 mph
Range: 500 miles
Armament: Two 20-mm cannon, two 7.9-mm
machine guns

MESSERSCHMITT BF.109G
Engine: 1475-hp Daimler Benz
Span: 32', 6"
Length: 29', 8"
Gross weight: 7500 lbs.
Top speed: 387 mph
Range: 615 miles
Armament: Three 20-mm cannon, two 13-mm
machine guns

MESSERSCHMITT 262 STORMBIRD
Engine: Two Junkers Jumo turbojet, 1980
lbs. thrust
Span: 40', 11"
Length: 34', 9"
Gross weight: 14,101 lbs.
Top speed: 540 mph
Range: 652 miles
Armament: Four 20-mm cannon

JAPAN

MITSUBISHI S–00 ZERO
Engine: 1120-hp Nakajima radial
Span: 36', 1"
Length: 29', 9"
Gross weight: 6026 lbs.
Top speed: 346 mph
Range: 1107 miles
Armament: Two 20-mm cannon, four 7.9-mm
machine guns

RECOMMENDED READING

Caidin, Martin
The Ragged, Rugged Warriors
E. P. Dutton and Company
New York, 1966

Constable, Trevor and Toliver, Colonel Raymond T.
Fighter Aces
The Macmillan Company
New York, 1966

Cooke, David C.
Fighter Planes that Made History
G. P. Putnam's Sons
New York, 1958

Godfrey, John T.
The Look of Eagles
Random House, Inc.
New York, 1958

Galland, Adolf
The First and the Last
Henry Holt and Company
New York, 1954

Hall, Grover C. Jr.
1,000 Destroyed
Morgan Aviation Books, Inc.
Dallas, 1959

Johnson, Group Captain J. E.
Wing Leader
Chatto and Windus, Ltd.
London, 1956

Johnson's Robert S. (with Martin Caidin)
Thunderbolt!
Ballantine Books, Inc.
New York, 1959

Luukaanen, Eino
Fighter Over Finland
MacDonald and Company, Ltd.
London, 1963

Stafford, Commander Edward P.
The Big E
Random House, Inc.
New York, 1962

INDEX

Republic P-47 Thunderbolt, 76, 79, 82, 85, 93–99, 101, 111
Rommel, Field Marshal Erwin, 54, 59, 63

S
Smith, Maj. John L., 130
Springs, Elliott White, 43–44
SB-2, 15
Stuka (see Junkers 87)
Supermarine Spitfire, 29–30, 38, 45, 49
Swett, Lt. James E., 132–134

T
Thach, Lt. Cmdr. John S., 123

U
U.S.S. *Hornet*, 126
U.S.S. *Lexington*, 122–123, 125
U.S.S. *Yorktown*, 126–128

V
von Richthofen, Wolfram, 7–8

W
Winston, Lt. Robert A., 18

Y
Yamamoto, Adm. Isorko, 133

A NOTE ABOUT THE AUTHOR

HERBERT MOLLOY MASON, JR. was born in Texas, but has lived much of his life in New York and in Europe. During and after World War II he served as a U.S. Marine aboard heavy warships, including the aircraft carriers U.S.S. *Midway* and *Franklin D. Roosevelt*. A graduate of both Trinity University and the American University of Beirut, Mr. Mason's interest in aviation dates back to his childhood. He has flown such diversified aircraft as Piper Cubs, Me-108s, B-17s, T-38 supersonic trainers, F-100s while a guest of the *Thunderbirds* and F-105s of Tactical Air Command.

Mr. Mason is the author of numerous books and magazine articles. For his work on THE NEW TIGERS: *The Making of a Modern Fighter Pilot,* published by McKay in 1967, the author was made an honorary pilot in the U.S. Air Force, one of the few such awards ever given.